MW01124980

SAKÉ

HEALTH AND LONGEVITY

SAKÉ

HEALTH AND LONGEVITY

BY YUKIO TAKIZAWA, M.D.

Veronica Lane Books
www.veronicalanebooks.com
email: *etan@veronicalanebooks.com*
2554 Lincoln Blvd. Ste 142, Los Angeles, CA 90232 USA
Tel/Fax: +1 (800) 652-2002 / Intl: +1 (310) 745-0262

HB ISBN: 978-0-9826513-7-7
Pbk ISBN: 978-0-9826513-8-4

Library of Congress Cataloging-in-Publication Data

The Library of congress No. 2006933160

93 p. cm

Summary: A scientific data-based treatise of the health benefits of the Japanese national alcohol drink Sakė with historical and cultural references.

Table of Contents

List of Figures, Tables and Glances

Foreword

Alcohol is a natural product that is obtained by fermenting sugars by yeasts. Man has adapted it as a popular social beverage and as an intoxicating drink since the beginning of history. Unfortunately, the widely held notions on the effects of alcohol on the human body go well beyond objective science. The Japanese, however, have always referred to their national alcoholic beverage as the "best medicine" with ten virtues. Saké not only serves as a tasty drink but also facilitates good physical and mental health, prompts conversation, and generally helps everyone get along well with each other. But saké is certainly more than just another alcoholic beverage. Saké is often referred to in Japanese as *kokushu*, meaning 'national beverage,' and has historically played a central role in Japanese culture.

Recent advances in medicine and related sciences explain how alcoholic beverages in general may contribute to the prevention of a variety of diseases. Moderate consumption of alcohol, for instance, is well established to protect one against coronary heart disease. Saké too offers a number of particular health benefits, including increased HDL (or the good) cholesterol, thus preventing heart attacks, strokes and other health problems. Furthermore, saké contains many naturally occurring nutrients.

The variety and the levels of amino acids found in saké are known to be much higher than in any other alcoholic beverage anywhere in the world. In light of the best current medical knowledge, moderate saké consumption is good for liver health, effective in preventing most forms of cancer, enables good blood flow, and reduces stress. A recent headline in an English-language newspaper I recently saw read "A drink a day, keeps the doctor away." I agree wholeheartedly!

High quality water and a fine grade of rice are essential ingredients for making quality saké. These are available in ample quantities in most regions of Japan. The other keys to producing superior saké include *koji* microbes, saké yeast, and skilled *toji* brewery workers. A good team spirit among the employees of the brewery is essential to success. When all these ingredients come together in a single location the resulting saké is natural, pure and clear. This is the highest quality saké and really good for one's health.

The Japanese Saké Brewers' Association is very pleased to recommend this book to all readers. In the book, the renowned author reviews current scientific knowledge on the potential health benefits of long-term moderate saké consumption. We thank Professor Y. Takizawa, of the Akita University School of Medicine, for thoroughly researching this topic and bringing his findings to the public, thereby stimulating both academic and popular interest in saké. I am grateful to Dr. Takizawa for his significant contribution and we take particular pleasure in acknowledging the importance of this book.

Toshihiko Asami, President,
Japanese Saké Brewers' Association
Tokyo, Japan 2010

Introduction

A truly unique and certainly a memorable experience for any visitor to Japan would be to sample the delicate taste of rice wine or saké. Japanese rice wine, the country's renowned national alcoholic beverage, brewed from rice (the staple food of Japan), has played a central role in the life, culture and even the religion of Japan. While the origins of saké can be traced back to China about 4,000 years ago, once introduced to Japan the brew developed its own characteristically Japanese variations. Today's Japanese saké is a distinctively different product from the Chinese rice wines bearing the same generic name. With some 2,000 Japanese breweries today producing over 10,000 brands of the brew, Japanese saké manufacture is indeed a healthy industry. The domestic Japanese consumption of saké in 2006 was estimated at 688,403 kiloliters (181,856,833 gallons) according to the Japan National Tax Administration.

Saké is different from other brewed alcoholic beverages in that it is produced in a two-step fermentation process. Unlike grape-based conventional wines that are fermented in a single step process, rice used in saké-making has to be first hydrolyzed into sugars (or saccharized) and then made into the wine in a second step. Rice lacks the tinted phyto-pigments abundant in grapes that deeply color the wine; saké is therefore generally colorless or very lightly tinted. The microbial mix of saké yeast is called *koji*. The yeast used in the process includes microbes such as Rhizopus and Sacharomycopsis, which secrete amylase proteins that convert product-fermented starch into sugar.

The ethanol content of saké varies widely with the variety of rice used and the particular manufacturing process employed, but typically ranges from 14% to 15% by volume. Depending on the variety, saké can contain about 120 different nutrients, including sugars, amino acids, organic acids and vitamins. The degree to which the rice is polished and how it is fermented determines the types and quantities of the nutrients present in the brew.

Consuming saké in moderation has been hailed in Japan since ancient times as a healthy practice that delivers good health, longevity and excellent skin tone. The unusually smooth, clear skin tones of brewery workers as well as the clear blemish-free skin of women from areas known for saké brewing are legendary in Japan. Local folklore often associates consumption of saké with the marked longevity of the connoisseurs of the brew. However, the role of saké in Japanese lifestyle is sometimes misunderstood and misinterpreted. Moderate drinking of saké regularly is beneficial to good health. The keyword, however, is "moderate." In fact, an ancient Japanese saying reminds the gourmet "to drink sake, not to get drunk by it."

Historic Japanese writings chronicle the "Ten Merits of Saké," which include the following: 1) the best medicine, 2) a means to prolong one's life, 3) a meal for a traveler, 4) a jacket against the cold, 5) an excuse to visit someone without an invitation, 6) a disperser of sorrow, 7) a social leveler, 8) a relief from work 9) a harmonizer of all men, and 10) a friend to those who live alone.

Conventional wisdom has always maintained that an alcoholic aperitif aids in digestion and assimilation of a meal. That moderate consumption of alcohol contributes to good health is consistent also with recent medical findings that suggest that a glass or two of wine daily aids in alleviating or preventing heart disease, a view that has been widely promoted by Western medicine in the past decade. Moderate use of alcoholic beverages acts indirectly to decrease the risk of cardio-vascular disease through the inhibition of oxidation of low-density lipoprotein, or via the reduction of coagulation processes. Moderate routine consumption of saké in particular has been shown to control the incidence of chronic diseases, including cardiac problems, diabetes, cancers, osteoporosis and senile dementia. Two recent Japanese studies support this claim about the healing effects of saké consumption on cancer. Generally, saké consumption was found to reduce the risk of most cancers except esophageal cancer.

A drink or two of saké with friends provides a soothing social diversion at the end of a stressful work day. In Japanese culture an evening drink of saké with a friend or a business acquaintance is a very common practice. These sessions nearly always lead to a better personal relationship, and can often be conducive to advantageous working relationships. It is not an exaggeration to say that in Japan more business decisions are likely to be made in these relaxed social settings than in formal business meetings at the office. Both the medical and psychological benefits of enjoying a daily drink of saké or even other wines are generally accepted to be a significant preventative measure against stress-induced or life style-related ailments. Saké is indeed the 'best medicine,' both medically and culturally.

This book is intended to inform the reader of the valuable characteristics of this uniquely soothing beverage and to establish its health benefits in preventing the incidence of the life-style related diseases inevitable in modern living. As saké is inextricably linked in Japanese society and culture, this book also attempts to portray some of the beneficial aspects of both saké and the Japanese lifestyle to the non-Japanese reader.

Chapter 1: Japanese Saké for Good Health

1.1. What is the Brewed Alcoholic Beverage Saké?

In the Japanese language the word saké is also a generic term used to mean alcohol. The correct Japanese term for refined rice wine is *seishu*, or more commonly *nihonshu*, although the term saké is used in common practice.[1] As already mentioned, saké is a very different beverage from grape-based wines. Unlike wine, saké is not aged or stored over long periods. It is generally consumed within a year or so of brewing.

The production cycle for high-quality saké also takes about a year. Usually, rice from the autumn crop is used for the process, which begins in winter and ends the following spring. The brew matures during the summer and is finally bottled in the autumn. Japanese saké is classified into different types and grades depending on the milling process used on the rice and any additives that might be employed in its brewing. With thousands of small breweries producing a rich variety of saké, finding one to suit one's palate shouldn't be a problem.

The alcohol content of saké is comparable to that of wine, generally around 16%. Recently, a new variety with a lower alcohol content in the range of 8-10% was introduced into the Japanese market to accommodate the growing preference among consumers for "light" saké. While it can be served either warmed or chilled, the cheaper varieties that are usually served warm (*atsukan*), straight into a glass in cheaper drinking establishments like *izakaya* or *yakitoriya*. Otherwise saké is served in an earthenware bottle (*tokkuri*) and poured into small cups (*sakazuki*).

1.1.1. General Health Effects of Saké

In Japan, many adults enjoy a daily serving of saké. The Japanese believe that the beverage provides key nutrients essential to maintaining good health, helps in the prevention of diseases, and facilitates relaxation or reduction of stress. Regular adult saké drinkers in Japan were estimated to be 43% of the population in 1965, and up to 67% in 1990. The annual amount of alcohol (mostly saké) consumed by one adult was 5.8 liters (6.13 quarts) in 1965 and 8.3 liters (8.77 quarts) in 1990.[2] Heavy drinkers are defined as those consuming 150ml (.63 cups) of pure alcohol per day or more. Today, it is estimated that there are more than six-million habitual drinkers in Japan. The belief in the significant beneficial biological effects of saké on human health is one of the main reasons for attracting so many saké consumers in Japan.

Alcoholic beverages can be broadly classified into two groups, brewed varieties such as beer or wine, and distilled spirits. Saké, like other wines, is considered to be a brewed beverage. In contrast, shochu, whisky, brandy, and vodkas are distilled liquors, and contain a much higher percent alcohol. Saké made primarily from staple food rice and water can be classified into the following four varieties in terms of taste and aroma:

1) Flavorful saké called *Ginjyo-shu*
2) Light, smooth saké called *Honjyozo-shu*

---

[1] *Kondo, H., Saké: A Driker's Guide. Tokyo, New York, London, Kodansha International Ltd., (1984).*

[2] *Japanese Ministry of Health and Welfare, Food whose intake changes greatly from year to year, 1990.*

3) Rich saké called *Junmai-shu*
4) Aged saké called *Jyukusei-shu*

Ginjyo-shu and *Honjyozo-shu* grades have brewed alcohol added to the *moromi*, a thick mash left to undergo slow fermentation with bacteria, yeasts and molds. We can also add the new type of light saké with lower alcohol content to the above list.

Since alcohol is easily dissolved in water and fat, it displays a strong affinity to body tissue and cells (such as nerve cells and nerve fibers) and therefore directly affects the central nervous system. Saké's pharmacological effects are similar to those of ethanol; namely, sedation, sleep, and anesthesia, all in common with mildly narcotic drugs. However, responsible moderate consumption of saké dose not result in drunkenness or alcoholism. Instead, it bestows a variety of benefits on body functioning as a physiological stimulant that prevents lifestyle-related diseases.

Consumption of alcohol (ethanol) has significant chorological effects. It can: 1) inhibit the vasomotor center and dilate peripheral blood vessels, thereby promoting heat transfer; 2) stimulate the oral cavity and gastric mucous membrane, thereby increasing heart rate; 3) stimulate the gastric mucous membrane, increasing the secretion of gastric juices; 4) Inhibit the anti-diuretic hormone activity in the pituitary gland, increasing the frequency of excretion of urine; and 5) cause sexual hyperesthesia. Although water is lost as a result, sodium (Na), potassium (K), and chlorine (Cl) are concentrated in the blood. This increases thirst and encourages further intake of water.

It is well known that habitual drinkers are usually hearty eaters. Unlike distilled liquor, the nature of saké has been shown to stimulate the gastric mucous membrane, thereby increasing the extra secretion of gastric juices. Gastrine is one of the components of gastric juice, and plays an important role in stomach physiology, such as increasing the thickness of the walls of the stomach. Gastrine is also secreted by eating soups containing meat or fish. For simple reasons, eating more soup increases more gastrine. However, eating too much soup can upset the stomach. Drinking saké will help relieve the discomfort. Saké as a part of appetizers at meals is a custom that aids digestive functions.[3]

1.1.2. Nutrients in Saké

In Figure 1 we show some of the main classes of the 120 different nutrients such as amino acids, amines, organic acids, sugars, vitamins that are typically found in saké. Unlike distilled liquors such as whiskey or *shochu*, the unique flavors of saké, are in part due to the amino acid content.

[3] *Fujita, T., "Cho wo kangaeru." Iwanami-shinsho, p.146, (1991).*

General Ingredients

Proteins

Gross protein	0.25%
Peptides	173.7mg
Sugars	2.18%

Vitamins

Folic acid	0.13mg
Vitamin B	0.31mg
Pantothenic acid	134.4mg
Biotin	1.67mg
Inositol	71.6mg
Cellulose	2.7mg

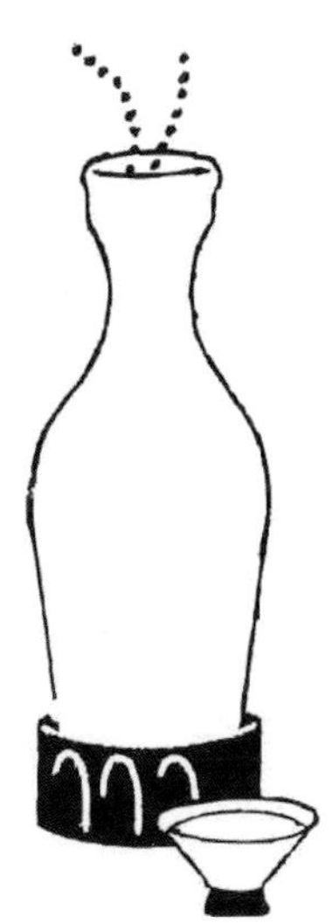

Specific Ingredients

Amino Acids (mg)

Tryptophan	
Lysine:	24.1
Histidine:	7.63
Arginine:	43.24
Asparticacid	1
Threonine:	7.74
Serine:	13.03
Glutamic acid:	30.89
Proline:	22.1
Glycine:	19.46
Alanine:	36.81
Cystine:	10.22
Valine:	17.30
Methionine:	2.21
Isoleucine:	9.22
Leucine:	22.0
Tyrocine:	17.44
Phenylalanine:	13.21

The analysis was carried out by Tokyo University of Agricultural using the Gakki Masamune of Honjyo-shu developed by Oki Daikiti Honten Brewery (Shirakawa, Fukushima).

Figure 1: The composition and nutrients known to be present in Japanese saké.

The typical concentration of the amino acids is in the range of range 10-200mg per 100ml. These amino acids have a wide range of biological effects on our bodies. For example, glutamic acid, alanine and leucine have great beneficial effects on our brain function, immune system, and protein metabolism. However, these amino acids and sugars are almost undetectable in distilled liquor.

1.2. Alcohol Metabolism

Alcohol can be absorbed in the stomach as well as in the small intestine at levels of 20% and 80%, respectively. The rate of absorption can be higher in on an empty stomach and increases with a higher concentration alcoholic drink. Within 1-2 hours of drinking, the alcohol is distributed into all of the organs and most of it is readily oxidized into carbon dioxide and water through the liver. The internal metabolic pathway of alcohol is shown in Figure 2. Via dehydration, alcohol is converted into acetaldehyde, which has a major impact on drunkenness. The acetaldehyde is further oxidized into acetic acid. This process has been called the microsomal ethanol oxidizing system.[4]

---

[4] *Lieber, C.S. & Carli, DE, Ethanol oxidation by hepatic microsomes: Adaptive increase after ethanol feeding, Science, 162, p. 917, 1968.*

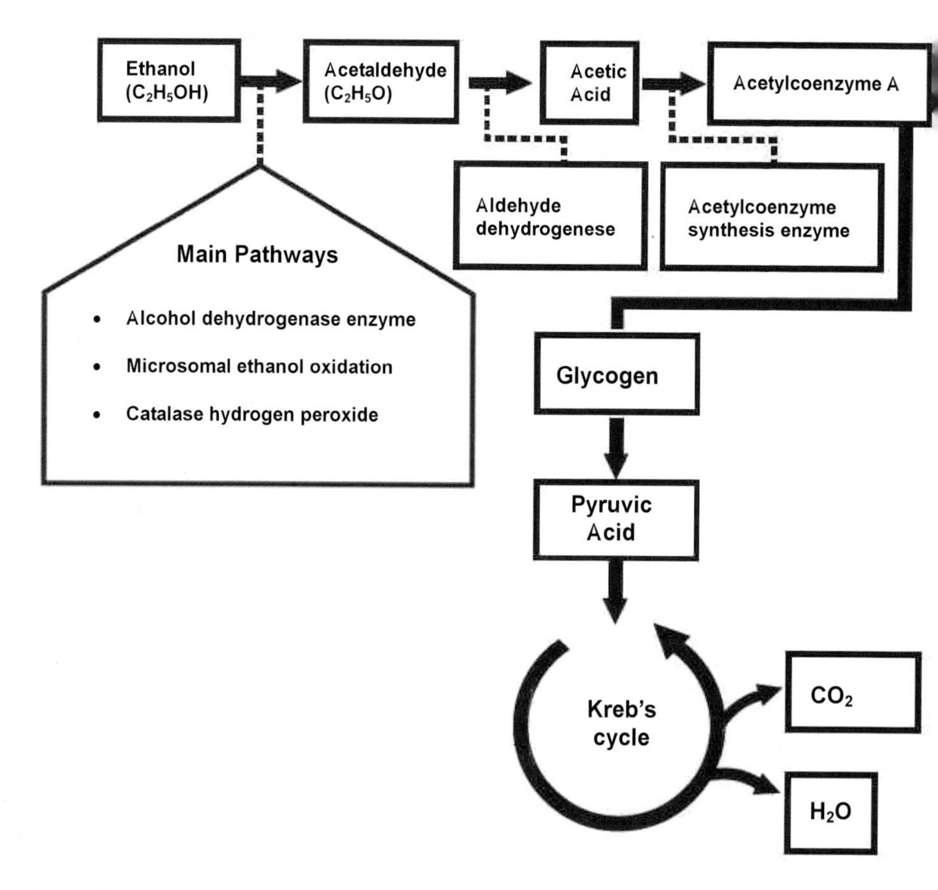

Ethanol is quickly destroyed in the body and converted largely to CO_2. Acetaldehyde and acetic acid are intermediates in this oxidation. This figure shows the effects of oxidation of ethanol on intermediated metabolism in the liver. The pathways inhibited by ethanol are represented by "Main systems" in broken box.

Figure 2: Metabolic pathway for alcohol (ethanol) in humans.

Alcohol concentration in blood is primarily dependent on the rate of intake of alcohol. Figure 3 shows alcohol and acetaldehyde concentrations in the blood of an adult who consumed 5 Japan *go* (one *go* is 180ml, or .01 oz) of saké. Blood alcohol concentration (BAC) peaks within 1-2 hours, and then deceases dramatically in a time-dependent manner until finally BAC decreases to zero levels after 12 hours. In contrast, the removal of acetaldehyde from the system is delayed up to 5 hours, compared to alcohol, but thereafter deceases at the same rate as alcohol.

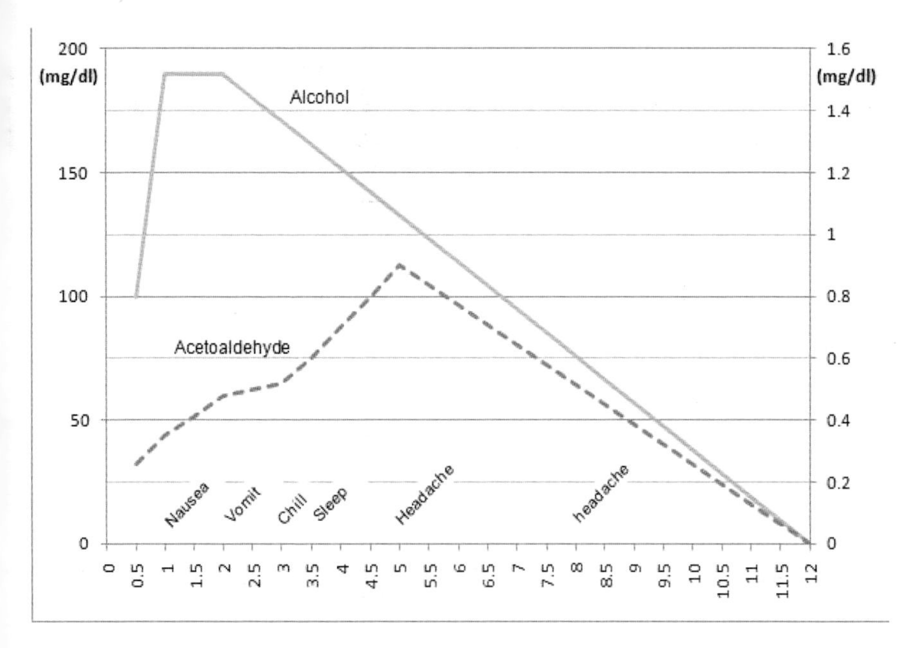

Five *go* (970ml) of saké was administered for half hour periods. In a 59-kg man, it would require approximately 10-12 hours to achieve a normal alcohol level in blood. The alcohol-dissembling capability differs from person to person. That means alcohol from one *go* of saké (180ml, 22g ethanol) will take three to four hours to be completely dissembled in the liver.

(From Akahane, J. & Nakanishi, E., 1970)

Figure 3: The change in blood concentration of ethanol and aldehyde over time since consuming alcoholic beverage.

1.3. Stress-relief by Saké

The concept of stress-relief by alcohol has been studied intensively in order to better appreciate the mechanisms of the interactions between stress and alcohol. Of particular interest is ascertaining if the stress-reducing effect of alcohol actually serves as a motivation for consumption.

Increasing evidence suggests that stress is at the root of many human diseases. Stress, especially work-related stress, affects the human organism through various psychological processes. Stress influences workers' health and well being through four types of closely interrelated mechanisms-: emotional, cognitive, behavioral, and physiological. Prolonged stress over time results in excessive wear-and-tear on the body and leads to impaired immunity, arteriosclerosis, obesity, bone demineralization, and the atrophy of the nerve cells in the brain. The brain controls the physiological and behavioral responses to daily events and stressors. Work-related social structures and processes can also often lead to stress.

Saké contains numerous amino acids, and stress-reducing effects result from the consumption of these amino acids. Alcohol significantly affects neuronal networks within the brain. There are two important brain-related amino acids in saké; namely, dopamine and the tyrosine-precursor serotonin, which both stimulate or inhibit emotions produced in the brain. The balance between these two amino acids is critical for normal brain function. For, instance, excessive dopamine levels or a deficiency in serotonin can cause irrational emotional behaviors that the brain is unable to control.

It is well known that a refreshing drink of saké can often release psychological stressor and this is why reserved or depressed persons become more talkative and exhibit increased social interaction on consuming saké.

1.4. Sleep Disorders and Saké

People spend one-fourth of their lifetimes sleeping. Dreaming accounts for approximately 20% of the total sleeping time. Sleeping is divided into two types, the so-called REM (rapid eye movement) sleep, which is shallow sleep with dreams, and non-REM sleep, which is more representative of deep sleep. Normal sleep includes both these. In the morning hours REM sleep, sleeping with dreams becomes predominant.[5]

Sleep is a vital and highly organized complex physiological process regulated by neuronal networks of the brain. Restful sleep plays an important role in our physiology, good health and longevity. Individual sleep patterns change with age and are easily susceptible to external and internal disruption. Reduction or disruption of sleep can affect a range of bodily functions, varying from thermoregulation to learning and memory loss.

Moderate consumption of saké is known to reduce REM sleep and increase the non-REM or deep sleep, therefore helping to make for more restful sleep. According to an important study by Dr. Gibson (London University), normal patterns of fluid and food intake are disturbed when the sleep–wake cycle is disrupted. The protein and carbohydrate sugar content in foods can also be affected during sleep. For example, a low protein-high carbohydrate sugar diet encourages sleep more than a high protein-low carbohydrate sugar diet.

Interestingly, saké is an ideal low protein-high carbohydrate sugar alcoholic beverage with only 0.25% protein but with as high as 22% carbohydrate sugars. Therefore it stimulates restful sleep. In addition, saké can stimulate the important brain hormone endorphin, which modulates emotion and also contributes to restful sleep

1.5. Amino Acids in Saké

Of the 120 different nutritional ingredients in saké, amino acids are probably the single-most important biological ingredients that help curb many lifestyle-related diseases. As shown in Figure 4, while saké contains many nourishing natural ingredients such proteins, carbohydrates, vitamins, and dietary fibers, it is particularly rich in important amino acids. As mentioned, saké is unique in this regard among alcoholic beverages. Modern brewing techniques make it possible to preserve most of the natural amino acids of the raw materials in saké.

---

[5] *Rechschaffen A. & Kales, A., Washington DC; Public Health Science US Government Printing Office (1968).*

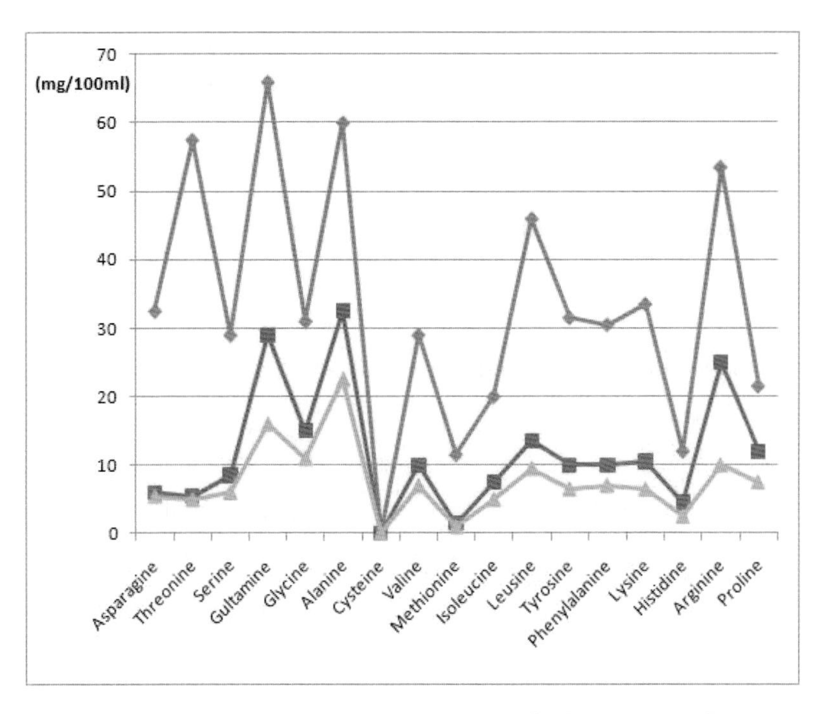

(From Oki Daikiti Honten Brewery, 2001)

Figure 4: Amino acids present in Ryori-shu, Junmai-shu and Futsu-shu (Saké).

Amino acids also play a critical role in crafting the delicate taste of the beverage. Individual amino acids are well known to elicit specific taste sensations. Sweetness is controlled by glycine, alanine, praline, and serine content; bitterness is controlled by phenylalanine, tyrosine, arginine, isoleucine, valine, methionine, and lysine; sourness is controlled by aspartic acid and glutamic acid.

There are near 300 amino acids in nature. However, all living organisms such as humans, animals, plants, and all microorganisms have only 20 different amino acids. Among them, e amino acids, so called essential amino acids, cannot be synthesized by the organism and must therefore be obtained from foods such as meat, fish, eggs, milk, and legumes. The amounts of amino acids in saké may vary in different brands. However, it is estimated that saké contains 10-20mg of amino acids in 100ml saké. The high amount of amino acids in saké is one of the unique features of saké, which provides a great rich and great-tasting source of essential amino acids.

1.5.1. Specific Amino Acids found in Saké

Amino acids are the basic organic molecules that form proteins. Proteins are fundamental components of all living cells and include many substances, such as enzymes, hormones, and antibodies—all necessary for the proper functioning of an organism.[6] We now review the biological functions of some of the key amino acids found in saké.

Alanine: Alanine is found in a wide variety of foods, but it is found at a particularly high level in saké. It is one of the simplest of the amino acids and is involved in the energy-producing breakdown reactions of glucose. Under conditions of sudden anaerobic energy demand, when muscle proteins are broken down for energy, alanine acts as a carrier molecule that takes the nitrogen-containing amino group to the liver for excretion. There it is changed into the less toxic urea, thus preventing buildup of toxic products in the muscle cells themselves undergoing catabolism when extra energy is needed. Alanine is also known to increase the immune response.

Arginine: Arginine is an essential amino acid that is especially needed when the body is under stress or is in an injured state. Stunted growth can result from the lack of dietary arginine. The secretion of human growth hormone and the physiology that works to suppress tumors are largely affected by arginine. Supplementation of arginine in the diet inhibits development of cancerous tumors that are both chemically-induced and naturally occurring.

Glutamine: Glutamine is found both as free amino acids and in the proteins contained in saké. Glutamine participates in immune response as well as in protein metabolism.

Valine: Valine has a stimulant effect. Healthy growth depends on the availability of valine and it is therefore used by athletes for encouragement of muscle growth, tissue repair, and as an energizer. It helps restore muscle mass in people with liver disease, serious injuries, or who have undergone surgery. Because valine cannot be produced by the body, healthy people should ensure that they are obtaining at least the recommended amount of it in their diet.

Proline: Proline is abundant in the major building materials of human body such as skin.

Lysine: Lysine is an essential amino acid that plays an important structural and chemical role in proteins. Lysine also participates in detoxification of body tissue.

Leucine: Leucine participates in alcohol metabolism and protects liver damage by toxic chemicals.

---

[6] *Kamiya, T., Biological function and health benefits of amino acids, FRI Journal, No.206, 2002.*

1.6. Overweight Problems, Obesity and Saké Consumption

Can drinking alcohol make you overweight? In the United States in 2003, the percentage of overweight people (as defined by a Body Mass Index (BMI) beyond 26; BMI equals weight divided by height-squared) nearly reached levels of 31.7% for males and 34.0% for females.[7] The health risks of obesity are well studied and obvious. Hypertension, type-2-diabetes, cancer and cardiovascular diseases are more prevalent and cause more mortality in overweight individuals. A BMI of 40 confers clinical obesity, a situation dangerous to life. Obesity and associated diseases are responsible for a large part of the health care budget in all Western countries, making it a major concern in these countries. Alcohol accounts for about 5.6 percent of the energy intake in the average American diet and up to 10 percent of the total energy in regular consumers of alcohol.

Although alcohol itself doesn't contain fat, it is packed with calories. And when mixers are used – juice, sugar and other ingredients – the calories can really add up. Alcohol seems to have a tendency to increase the BMI, depending on the pattern of intake. The overall, habitual consumption of alcohol in excess of energy needs probably favors lipid storage and weight gain and may thus contribute to obesity and overweight.

Although we have known for some time that excess weight is an important factor in death from many chronic diseases, our knowledge of the relationship between alcohol consumption and obesity is limited. Reported findings on the protective effect of light-to-moderate alcohol consumption against obesity have been controversial.

Recently, some studies suggest that alcohol consumption may not be as "fattening" as traditionally believed and that the contribution of alcohol to the BMI of the population is very minor. The evidence comes from the American Nurses' Health Study,[8] which investigated the height, weight, and drinking and eating patterns of 90,000 women aged 30 to 55. One would expect that those who consumed extra calories through regular drinking of alcohol would be overweight. But this was not found to be the case. The most overweight group consisted of women who didn't drink at all. And up to a rate of several drinks a day, the higher consumption correlated with lower body weight.

1.7. Athletic Value of Saké

Many studies have shown that people who drink moderate amounts of saké for decades remain "as healthy as a horse" until they die of "natural causes".[9, 10] Drinking as little as 2 ounces saké per night with dinner is enough to bring benefits. The crucial role of muscle glycogen used as a fuel during prolonged exercise is well established. The effects of acute changes in dietary carbohydrate intake on muscle glycogen content and on endurance capacity are also equally well known.

---

[7] *Ogden, C.L., et al., Prevalence of overweight and obesity in the United States, JAMA, 295, p.1549, 2006.*

[8] *Williamson, P., et al., Alcohol and body weight in the United States Adults, American J Public Health, 77, 1324, 1987.*

[9] *Nakayama M., et al., "Alcohol to Kenkou", alcohol Kenkou Igaku kyokai, http://www.arukenkyo.or.jp/*

[10] *Takizawa, Y., Health-Positive Effects of the 'Saké' of Japan. Foods & food ingredients (FFI) Journal of Japan, 208, p.955, 2003.*

Consumption of a low-to-moderate amount of saké increases the intake of necessary proteins for exercise.

Saké contains leucine, isoleucine, and valine, three critical amino acids for developing muscular power. In addition, saké also contains arginine, which has a critical function in the body's recovery from exercise-related muscle distress. The ability to optimize muscular power output is considered fundamental to success in athletic activities. Consequently, a great deal of research has investigated methods to improve prolonged athletic power output through proteins and nutritional products.

1.8. The Skin and Saké

Immunity is the protection of the body from disease caused by an infectious agent, such as a bacterium or virus. However, overreaction to immune-response can also damage our body and even promote immune-response-associated diseases. An allergy is a particularly good example of an abnormally high sensitivity to certain substances, such as pollens, foods, or microorganisms. Common indications of an allergy may include sneezing, itching, and skin rashes. Recently one often hears the word "atopy," which means an allergic reaction caused by a genetic predisposition toward developing hypersensitivity reactions, such as hay fever, asthma, or chronic urticaria, upon exposure to specific antigens.

1.8.1. Atopic Dermatitis

Atopic dermatitis is characterized by intense itching, and occurs in individuals predisposed to certain hypersensitivity reactions. Recent studies from Europe and the U.S. have shown that linolenic acid has a therapeutic effect on atopic dermatitis. In Japan, a research group from Hamamatsu Medical College extracted linoleic acid from herbs and confirmed the therapeutic effect of linolenic acid for this condition.[11] Although linoleic acid is a minor component of most diets, at present it is provoking intense scientific research. This is due to the range of potential health effects demonstrated by linoleic acid in animal and human studies including beneficial effects on body composition, a reduction in body fat mass, anticarcinogenicity, antidiabetogenicity, and especially immune modulating effects. Since saké contains linoleic acid, moderate drinking of saké would appear to have a positive effect in the treatment of atopic dermatitis.

1.8.2. Cosmetic Effects on Skin

The skin is the largest organ of the human body. It guards against external biological, chemical, and physical attack on the body, and also protects the body from water loss. The skin helps regulate body temperature and provides immunity. The skin comprises epidermis and dermis, contains hair follicles, sebaceous glands, sweat glands, and vascular components. The skin is more than an inert covering for the body. It is a living organ, and, in fact, outweighs the liver.

It is well known that women who live in the northern region of Japan, where there are high levels of saké consumption, tend to have particularly smooth skin

[11] *Takikawa, M. & Tanaka, T., "Atopic dermatitis no Shokuji Ryouhou. Kenkou-soku", Shukan Asahi, Asahi Shinbun-Sha, p.420 (2004).*

complexions. Therefore, generations of Japanese have appreciated the positive and beneficial effects of saké simply for its role in promoting skin health.

The use of saké sediment (*sakékasu*) in facial mask treatments is also beneficial for skin improvement. Face masks with *sakékasu* and various amino acids in them will produce smooth and velvety skin. A facial mask made with *sakékasu* (saké sediment) is shown in Glance 1.

1. Break down into pieces about 20 grams of *sakekasu* in a mortar and soak it in distilled water.
2. Pound the mixture down into paste.
3. Add half teaspoonful of flour and pound the mixture until you think it is sticky enough to
4. apply on the face. Apply the mixture on the face and about 15 minutes. Rinse it off gently.

(From "Nada no Sake for Health and Beauty")

Glance 1: Saké remains used as a beauty treatment.

Saké residues are good material for facial masking as amino acids, effective in hydrating the skin, are included in saké as well as in saké residues.

1.8.3. Skin Water-Loss Protection and Saké

Japanese people have used saké as a skin care lotion since ancient times. Recent studies agree that some amino acids isolated from saké are active ingredients for the protection of skin against potent environmental threats. A number of studies have shown that the amino acids isolated from saké help the skin perform these functions. Unlike other alcohol-containing products, a moderate serving of saké can accelerate skin blood circulation, as well as increase and maintain skin temperatures.

1.9. Sunburn and Sun Tan

Human skin is the only organ directly exposed to ultraviolet irradiation from the sun. Solar ultraviolet irradiation is a well-recognized, potent environmental harming agent capable of damaging skin and causing skin cancers. Ultraviolet irradiation-induced skin damage includes sunburn, immune suppression, cancer, and premature skin aging, also known as photo-aging. Recent studies have demonstrated that the topical application of saké concentrate suppressed damaging effects of solar ultraviolet radiation. Topical application of a saké concentrate significantly increased intercellular lipid and loricrin content, a protein found in the out layer of the skin, the stratum corneum.

The role of melanin in humans is to protect the skin from ultraviolet irradiation-induced damage. However, the overproduction of melanin in the skin may cause melasma, freckles, ephelides, hyperpigmentation, and age spots. As shown in Figure 5, melanin production is controlled by tyrosinase, a key enzyme for melanin synthesis. Tyrosinase catalyzes two distinct reactions of melanin synthesis, the hydroxylation of a monophenol, and the conversion of an o-diphenol to the corresponding o-quinone. The melanin pigment is generated as a result of spontaneous polymerization of the quinones.

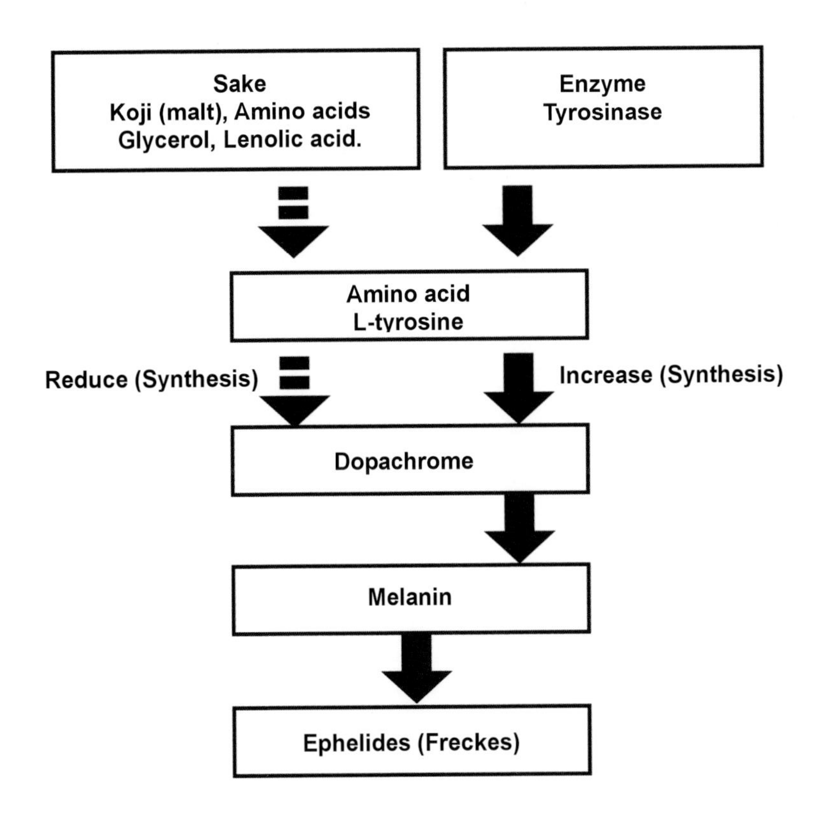

Protosensitization designates an abnormal adverse reaction to ultraviolet and/or visible radiation.

Figure 5: Synthetic pathway for Melanin.

In addition, tyrosinase has been reported to be associated with neurodegenerative diseases as well as Parkinson's disease. Therefore, the development of tyrosinase inhibitors has been anticipated in the food, pharmaceutical, and cosmetic industries. Some amino acids contained in saké have been shown to inhibit tyrosinase activity. Because these amino acids in saké function safely in this capacity, saké might prove useful for these protective applications in the cosmetic field.

1.10. Saké Bathing for Health

Skin cleansing is considered an important aspect of daily hygiene and also a potent therapy for skin disease. There are numerous skin cleanser products on the market with different modes of cleansing action (detergent or adsorptive) and with different levels of general and specific epidermal toxicity, ease of rinsing and variable amounts of additives (natural or synthetic), e. g. perfume oils.

In most cases, these products do an adequate job in removing dirt. What cannot be easily controlled are the adverse side effects inherent in the use of cleansing products. These side effects include: damage to the barrier function of the skin; increased susceptibility to environmental sources of irritation and sensitization; irritation responses, such as erythema and edema; and reduced cosmetic characteristics of the skin such as the degree of moisture and smoothness. Worse still, most of these changes are subtle, occurring slowly over a period of time.

The crucial advantage of a Japanese saké bath is not just that of a recommended skin cleanser but also as a great therapeutic agent for maintaining glowing and healthy skin.[12] Saké bathing is reported to provide relief from many chronic diseases and promote relaxation. It is a pampering comfortable luxury considered safe and well tolerated by most healthy adults.

Some studies have also suggested that long-term saké bathing may help lower blood pressure in patients with hypertension and improve their blood circulation. The transient improvements in pulmonary function that results from saké bathing may provide some relief to patients with asthma and chronic bronchitis. It may also alleviate pain and improve joint mobility in patients with rheumatic diseases. Saké bathing does not cause any drying of the skin. It may even benefit patients with psoriasis. In patients with atopic dermatitis itching increases as a result of increased sweating. Cutaneous circulation increases greatly during saké bathing in order to prevent overheating of the body.

In regular bathing, blood pressure tends to fall but this is countered by increased cardiac output that results from a faster heart rate and decreased blood flow to the visceral organs. Cooling the body in cold air, cold showers, water or rolling in snow causes rapid cutaneous vasoconstriction, leading to elevation of arterial blood pressure and increased central venous blood volume. These effects of both heat and cold are mediated via the sympathetic nervous system. The circulatory responses to saké bathing are related to the intensity and duration of the exposure. An ordinary saké bath also increases cardiac workload about as much as moderate or vigorous walking.

1.11. General Anti-Aging Effects of Moderate Alcohol Consumption

A number of studies have been shown that light-to-moderate alcohol consumption contributes to quality of life for the elderly. In the United States, wine is served in more than half the hospitals, and the "cocktail hour" is now part of the routine in most nursing homes. One of the best studies to identify the factors that contribute to a healthy, active old age was conducted in Alameda County, California, and published in the American Journal of Public Health in 1989.[13] 841 people born before 1920 were questioned about their health and activity patterns. Nineteen years later they checked on the survivors of this group, which had now been whittled down to 496 by death. These survivors, aged between sixty-five and eighty-nine, were asked about their everyday activities. 107 individuals, or about a quarter, were very healthy, and counted as "high-functioning."

One of the important factors that kept the spark alive in those high-functioning individuals was consuming moderate amounts of alcohol. Those with moderate

---

[12] *Imayasu, S.& Kawato, A., Effectiveness of Saké on Your Health & Beauty. Journal of the Brewing Society of Japan, 94, p. 274, 1999.*

[13] *Levenstein, C., Am J Public Health, 79, 11, 1989.*

alcohol intake were found to be 2.4 times more likely to have high function at the follow-up relative to abstainers and 1.7 times more likely to have high function relative to heavy drinkers.

Also interesting are the studies conducted by researchers from Indiana State and Duke Universities in the U.S.[14] Over a period of 20 years they have kept track of nearly four thousand twins who were veterans of the Second World War, keeping a careful tally on their drinking habits. The latest check on the cognitive skills of these men, now mostly in their sixties, seventies, or eighties, shows those who have one or two drinks a day score significantly higher that their brothers who either abstain or drink more or less than that amount. A study of six thousand Americans over sixty-five confirmed that moderate drinkers performed better in tests of their mental ability.

Even more surprising were the results of a study of bone mineral density in the elderly published in the British Medical Journal in 1993. Osteoporosis is a disease in which the bones become extremely porous, are subject to fracture, and heal slowly, occurring especially in women following menopause, and often leading to curvature of the spine from vertebral collapse. Osteoporosis is a major cause of disability as we get older.

Researchers from the University of California, San Diego, studied the bone mineral density of a group of 182 men and 267 women in the early 1970s when they were all over the age of forty-five, also making a note of their drinking habits. Sixteen to nineteen years later the same subjects were checked again, and the result showed that moderate drinkers had higher bone density levels. All these studies indicate that light-to-moderate alcohol consumption generally contributes to the quality of life for the elderly.

1.12. Cold Environment and Saké

The morphological and physiological differences between women and men largely affect thermoregulation during exposure to cold environments. One of the main physical differences affecting thermoregulation is the relatively higher surface-area-to-mass ratio in women. In a warm environment this allows them to rely more on dry heat loss and less on evaporative cooling. However, in cold environments, the greater surface-area-to-mass ratio results in a higher rate of heat loss. The lower body fat in women compared to that in men provides lower insulation and presents a disadvantage in a cold environment. The main physical difference between women and man affecting thermoregulation is women's unique endogenous organs, the uterus and ovaries. Since these organs need large volumes of blood, the relative blood supply to other organs is less in women compared with men.

For over a thousand years, ancient Japanese have believed that there was a link between saké and the cold environment. Recent studies have shown that moderate consumption of saké can maintain our body temperature in the cold. During acute exposure to a cold environment saké may prove advantageous by increasing blood circulation and heat production.

---

[14] *Christian, J.C., et al., Self-reported alcohol intake and cognition in aging twins, J Stud Alcohol, 56, p.414, 1995.*

1.13. Joint Stiffness/Pain and Saké

In the day-to-day clinical practice, shoulder stiffness and pain is clearly one of the most frequent complaints of the elderly. Responding to this complaint is difficult for doctors who have no simple successful treatment for this condition. In comparison to younger people, what is first noticeable about elderly people is that they have a lot of fat in the body and a markedly low level of intracellular water. In other words, they are at a comparatively higher risk of dehydration and liable to go into shock. Although the exact cause of shoulder stiffness and pain is not so clear, the dorsal roots in the elderly tend to degenerate, and this partially explains such complaints as neck and shoulder stiffness and pain. However, these complaints cannot be dismissed simply as "an unidentified syndrome." Behind these complaints is invariably one or another organic disorder.

Since saké increases blood circulation, it is anticipated that saké has a beneficial effect on shoulder stiffness and pain. Indeed, it has been shown that taking a saké bath is able to release shoulder stiffness and reduces pain successfully, presumably due to the amino acids and vitamins in saké that are absorbed by the skin.

Chapter 2: The Health Benefits of Saké

2.1. Long Term Benefits of Saké

2.1.1. Alcohol and Longevity

Moderate alcohol consumption increases the immune response in the brain by affecting a complex regulation process in the brain's neuronal networks. Longevity is based on a healthy immune system. The first scientific study on the possible benefits of moderate alcohol consumption on human health and immunity was reported in 1926 by biologist Raymond Pearl. His analysis of family historical data from the Baltimore, Maryland area suggested that that moderate drinkers exhibited greater longevity compared to non-drinkers or heavy drinkers (Pearle, 1926). Moderate drinking in this study meant that the amount of brewed or distilled alcohol consumed was not sufficient to cause intoxication.[15].

Naturally, Raymond Pearl's results went against the conventional beliefs and were criticized by several authors at the time. Interestingly, his initial studies were on chickens. In those studies birds that were administered alcohol far outlived those in the control group.

Modern understanding is consistent with Pearl's findings. Mortality from all causes is well established to be 21% to 28% lower among moderate drinkers than among abstainers.[16] The National Institute on Alcohol Abuse and Alcoholism (NIAAA) in 2004 completed an extensive review[17] of current scientific knowledge about the health effects of moderate alcohol consumption and concluded that moderate consumption is beneficial to heart health, resulting in a sharp decrease (40%-60%) in the risk of heart diseases. Numerous other studies agree with these conclusions. These studies include one on Italian men drinking 1-4 drinks per day (Farchi, 2000), another recent study on reduced mortality in 70-79 year olds (Maraldi et al., 2006), and an Australian study showing that abstainers were twice as likely to enter a nursing home compared to moderate drinkers (both men and women) (McCallum et al., 2003). The geographic diversity of these studies suggest that the phenomenon is not specific to certain ethnic groups.

A 1998 study in Honolulu (Maskarinec, 1998) also came up with similar conclusions; men who consumed from 1 to 28 drinks per week had a reduced risk for all-cause mortality of 14% to 22%. A more recent study reported by Gaziano et al., (1995) also found that moderate drinking was linked to longevity. Curiously, a United Kingdom study in 2001 estimated that the lives saved by moderate alcohol consumption were greater than the lives lost through abuse of alcohol during the same period.

Of the various lifestyle changes that might be adopted, moderate consumption of alcohol appears to be the most effective[18] in reducing the risk of heart failure and

---

[15] *His moderate category would have you drink "a daily pint or two of beer, or a daily bottle of claret, or a few glasses of whiskey."*

[16] *Camargo, C. A., et al., Prospective study of moderate alcohol consumption and mortality in US male physicians.* Archives of Internal Medicine, *157, 79, 1997.*

[17] *Highlights of the NIAAA position paper on moderate alcohol consumption. Press release from the journal,* Alcoholism: Clinical & Experimental Research, *June 14, 2004; Berman, J., Moderate alcohol consumption benefits heart, U.S. government says. Voice of America News, June 16, 2004.*

[18] *With smokers, however, giving up smoking is more effective.*

other diseases (Hanson, 2008). A host of health problems are claimed to be averted by the use of alcohol. The advantages appear to be applicable to both sexes and all age groups as confirmed by studies on women,[19], 45-65 year olds,[20] and 70-79 year olds[21]. Light to moderate consumption of alcohol appears to reduce the risk of coronary heart disease by as much as 80% among individuals with older-onset diabetes, according to a study published in the Journal of the American Medical Association.[22]

A study conducted in Netherlands (the Zutphen study)[23] is particularly interesting in this regard as it compared wine drinking with that of other alcoholic beverages. As expected, the study on 1373 men found a 36% lower relative risk of all-cause death and a 34% lower relative risk of cardiovascular death for moderate[24] consumers of alcohol compared to non-drinkers. With wine-drinkers in particular, however, the reduction was much greater, amounting to a 40% lower rate of all-cause death and a 48% lower incidence of cardiovascular death!

While factors such as age, sex, race, smoking, ethnic background, and education affect the relationship between alcohol consumption and human health, many studies carried out in different cultures around the world have found a common conclusion. Light-to-moderate alcohol consumption is associated with decreased total mortality, most of which were due to a reduction in cardiovascular disease-associated deaths.

2.1.2. Association between Alcohol Consumption and Mortality

The relationship between moderate alcohol consumption and all-cause mortality has been reported in several well-designed studies. Most reported data suggest a U-shaped or a J-shaped dependence of mortality on the extent of routine alcohol consumption. For instance, a recent review of all recent data concluded this relationship to be U-shaped, with a minimum point (corresponding to maximum benefits) around one drink per day.[25] This decreased overall mortality is largely associated with the beneficial effects of moderate alcohol consumption on reducing

---

[19] *Fuchs, C. S., et al., Alcohol consumption and mortality among women.* The New England Journal of Medicine, 332 (19), *1245, 1995.*

[20] *Farchi, G., et al., Alcohol and survival in the Italian rural cohorts of the Seven Countries Study.* International Journal of Epidemiology, 29, *667, 2000.*

[21] *Maraldi, C.,* et al., *Impact of inflammation on the relationship among alcohol consumption, mortality, and cardiac events: the Health, Aging, and Body Composition Study.* Archives of Internal Medicine, 166 (14), *1490, 2006.*

[22] *Valmidrid, C. T., et al., Alcohol intake and the risk of coronary heart disease mortality in persons with older-onset diabetes mellitus.* Journal of the American Medical Association, 282 (3), *239, 1999.*

[23] *The study was partly funded by a grant from the former Inspectorate for Health and Protection and Veterinary Public Health, which is presently integrated in the Food and Consumer Product Safety Authority, The Netherlands, and partly by the National Institute for Public Health and the Environment (RIVM), The Netherlands. Co-authors are Marga C. O.et al., (http://supercentenarian.com/archive/wine.html)*

[24] *defined in this study as consuming less than or equal to 20 grams per day (1 glass of alcoholic beverage contains 10 grams of alcohol, 1 ounce = ~30 mL of alcoholic beverage)*

[25] *Boffetta, P., and Garefinkel, L., Alcohol drinking among men enrolled in an American Cancer Society prospective study.* Epidemiology, 1 (5), *42, 1990.*

coronary heart disease. This U-shaped dependence of all-cause mortality on alcohol consumption was first proposed by Dr. Marmot, a British scientist, in 1981.

As shown in Figure 6, for the groups of light or moderate consumers of alcohol, the risk of all-cause mortality is much less than either non-drinkers or heavy drinkers. Surprisingly, the data are unrelated to individuals' smoking, blood pressure, blood cholesterol, and occupation. But a majority of these reports are from Western countries, and there is only rather limited evidence regarding the beneficial effects of alcohol consumption among other ethnic groups. However, a prospective study of Chinese men[26] showed that moderate alcohol consumption reduced the risk of total mortality compared with that for abstainers. Also, a US study[27] addressing this question found studies from at least 20 different countries that demonstrated a 20% to 40% lower coronary heart disease CHD incidence among drinkers compared to nondrinkers.

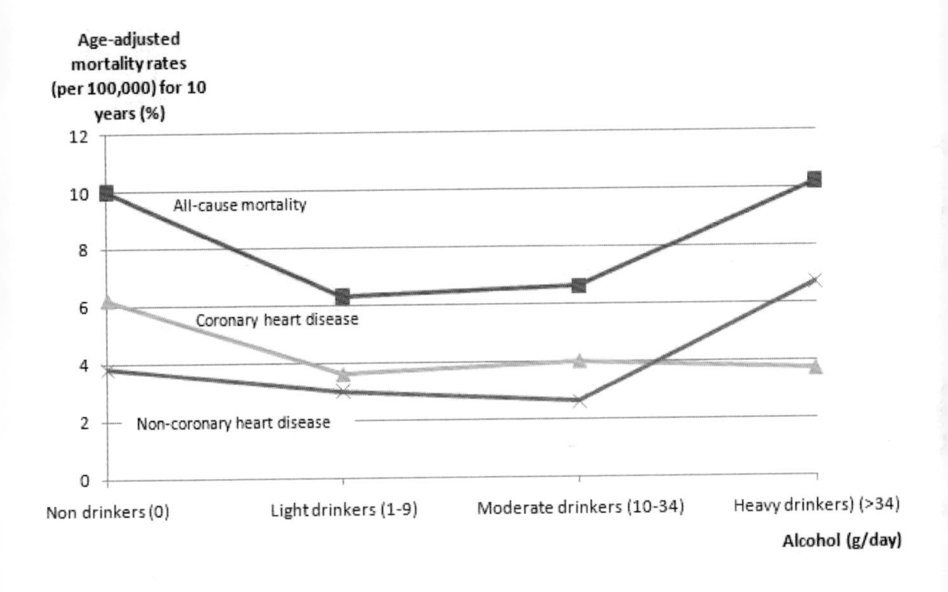

(From Marmot, M. G. et al., 1981)

Figure 6: The U-shaped curve depicting the relationship between regular alcohol intake and all-cause mortality as well as with coronary heart disease.

Findings from a well-known Japanese study, the Japan collaborative large cohort study sponsored by Monbusho (the JACC Study), was reported in 1990 by Professor Aoki of Nagoya University. The alcohol consumption by a total of 110,792

---

[26] Yuan, J-M., et al., *Follow up study of moderate alcohol intake and mortality among middle aged men in Shanghai, China.* British Medical Journal, 314, *18, 1997.*

[27] *Renaud, S., et al., Alcohol drinking and coronary heart disease. In: Verschuren, P.M., ed. Health Issues Related to Alcohol Consumption. Washington, DC: ILSI Press, 1993.p. 81: Klatsky, A.L., Epidemiology of coronary heart disease Influence of alcohol. Alcohol Clin Exp Res 18 (1): 88, 1994.*

Japanese men and women aged 40 to 79 years was recorded through December 31, 1999. The JACC Study indicated that the risk of all-cause mortality to be the lowest among current drinkers with an alcohol intake of 0.1 to 22.9 g/d (approximately 2 *go* drinks a day). A 12% to 20% decrease was reported for those who consumed less than 2 *go* (23 g/d) of alcohol, but heavy drinking increased that risk. This suggests the validity of the U-shaped relationship for this population as well. The benefits associated with light-to-moderate alcohol consumption were clearly apparent even among subjects aged 60 years or older.

The J-shaped relationship has also been observed. In 1990 through 1996 a similar study was conducted in four public health center areas as part of the Japan Public Health Center-based prospective study on cancer and cardiovascular disease (JPHC). In this study on 20,000 men aged 40-59 years the relationship between light-to-moderate alcohol consumption and all-cause mortality was found to be J-shaped. The general health of those who consumed alcohol in moderation was clearly superior to that of either the non-drinkers or the heavy drinkers. This protection against all-cause mortality was evident at drinking levels of up to two drinks a day in nearly all studies reported. However, excessive drinking and binge drinking is well-recognized as a risk factor for many diseases.

Any disparity in data on the effects of alcohol consumption on health or mortality can generally be interpreted as differences due to moderate versus heavy drinking. The same J-shaped dependence was also obtained in a French study by Drs. Renaud and Lorgeril carried out in 1992. Consuming moderate amounts of alcohol clearly reduced all-cause mortality, whereas when the consumption exceeded moderation, up to maybe more than 2-3 drinks a day, the risk of all-cause mortality also rose. This is illustrated in Figure 7. The more conservative J-shaped risk profile where the risk of mortality is high for heavy drinks is the more risk-averse theory.

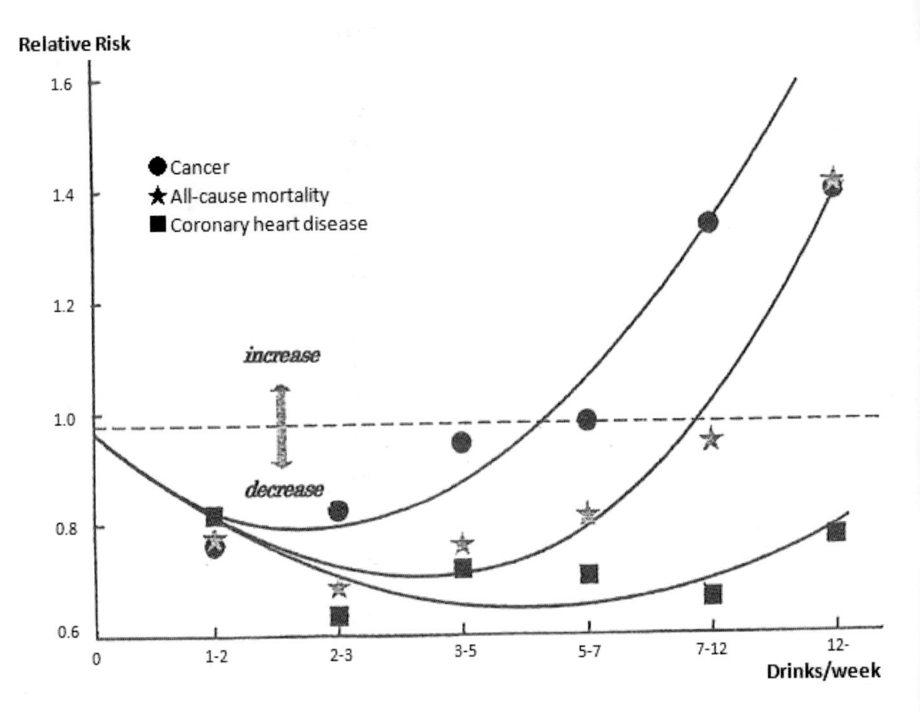

(From Renaud, S. D. & Lorgeri, M., 1992)

Figure 7: The J-shaped curve depicting the relationship between regular consumption of wine and all-cause mortality, cancer and coronary heart disease

Although the French diet is high in saturated fats the mortality rate from coronary heart diseases is low! This interesting phenomenon was first observed by Irish physician Samuel Black in 1819. Recently, Professor Renaud, an epidemiologist, referred to this phenomenon as the French Paradox, (the topic of a now famous broadcast of the U.S. news show 60 Minutes in November 1991). In 1998, Professor Renaud visiting Kobe, Japan to attend a WHO forum, delivered an impressive speech on wine and health. His speech catalyzed a large increase in the demand for red wines around Japan.

It is now believed that at least one of the active ingredients in wine, resveratrol, is primarily responsible for its positive health effects. Resveratrol and other grape phytocompounds have been positively linked to prevention of or even the reversal of cancer, heart disease, degenerative nerve disease, and other ailments. Consumption of red wine as opposed to white wine is considered more beneficial because many of these phytocompounds are found only in the outer skin of grapes and only red wine is fermented with the skins.

2.2. Fighting Arteriosclerosis

Arteriosclerosis refers to degenerative changes in the arteries, characterized by thickening of the walls of arteries. The thickening and hardening due to the accumulation of calcium results in a consequent loss in elasticity and therefore restricted blood flow. The condition is defined by the formation of plaques of cholesterol, platelets, fibrin, and other substances on the arterial walls. When the thickening is due to deposits of lipids, fatty substances and cholesterol the condition is called arteriosclerosis. This thickening of the arterial walls and leads to progressive degrees of blockage of the circulation.

The so-called Coronary Artery Disease (CAD) is due to the decreased blood flow in the coronary Artery that supplies the heart. Of the various possible causes for arteriosclerosis the most common is the deposition of plaques of cholesterol, platelets and other substances within the arterial walls. Sometimes the build-up is very slow and gradual but in other cases it can be sudden. Serious blockage of flow can occur when a chunk of the plaque matter breaks off and blocks the already narrowed lumen of a vessel. When the blood flow to the brain is restricted because of such blockage brain function is impaired and the victims suffer a stroke. Diet is the primary factor to be considered in preventing arteriosclerosis. One of the benefits of alcohol consumption was shown to be the reduction in the harmful arterial plaque build-up.[28]

2.2.1. Low-density Lipoprotein (LDL, Bad Cholesterol)

Low-density lipoprotein (LDL) is a complex of lipids and proteins, (usually with more lipid than protein) that transports cholesterol in the blood stream, usually from the liver to the peripheral tissues. It is commonly referred to as 'bad cholesterol' as high LDL levels potentially lead to cardiovascular disease. Because LDLs transport cholesterol in the blood flowing through the arteries, increased levels are associated with arteriosclerosis, and thus also with heart attack, stroke and peripheral vascular disease. However, it is not the cholesterol itself that is bad; rather it is the location, the rate at which it develops, and the form it is being transported in, that determine its ill effects. LDL poses a definitive risk for cardiovascular disease when it invades the endothelium and becomes oxidized. A complex set of biochemical reactions regulates the oxidation of LDL, chiefly stimulated by presence of free radicals in the endothelium.

On the other hand, high-density lipoprotein (HDL, good-cholesterol) is a complex of lipids and proteins in approximately equal amounts. HDL is believed to remove cholesterol from within the arteries and transport it back to the liver for excretion or reuse. It is therefore often called 'good cholesterol,' and high levels of HDL are usually associated with a decreased risk of arteriosclerosis and coronary heart disease.

---

[28] *A Vliegenthart, R.*, et al., *Alcohol consumption and coronary calcification in a general population.* Archives of Internal Medicine, 164, *2355, 2004.*

Moderate consumption of alcohol was shown[29] to decrease the incidence of bad or LDL cholesterol. Alcohol reduces heart attacks, ischemic strokes and circulatory problems through a number of identified ways (Hanson, 2008). It improves blood lipid profile by increasing HDL ("good") cholesterol and decreasing LDL ("bad") cholesterol. It decreases thrombosis (blood clotting) by reducing platelet aggregation, reducing fibrinogen (a blood clotter) and increasing fibrinolysis (the process by which clots dissolve). Other ways include such as increasing coronary blood flow, reducing blood pressure, and reducing blood insulin level.

2.2.2. Saké Increases High-density Lipoprotein (HDL, Good Cholesterol)

Numerous studies have shown that moderate wine or alcohol consumption is beneficial in fighting arteriosclerosis. The evidence is strong enough to conclude that moderate drinking helps protects one against any kind of stroke. One possible protective mechanism is via the increase in levels of 'good cholesterol' or HDL in the blood[30]. The particle size distribution of both LDL and HDL in the blood has a bearing on how easily they deposit on the vessel walls. This distribution pattern was also found to be improved by alcohol consumption.[31] Dr. Arthur Klatsky, a cardiologist in Oakland, California, reported in 1989 that people who consumed moderate alcohol every day were 25 percent less likely to have stroke than non-drinkers. The most important benefit is that moderate drinkers reduced their stroke-related risk by 60 percent compared to non-drinkers.

A recent study by Dr. Wakabayashi in Japan on investigating the effects of saké consumption on blood cholesterol demonstrated that moderate consumption resulted in lower level of bad cholesterol and higher level of good cholesterol compared to non-drinkers.

2.2.3. Saké and Blood Pressure

Hypertension, or high blood pressure, is the single-most important risk factor for stroke. It is a 'fire alarm' that warns of future medical complications. As the blood pressure builds up, the heart has to pump progressively harder to force the blood around our body, placing the organ itself as well as the arteries under greater

---

[29] *Numerous studies support this conclusion. A few are as follows: Paassilta, M.,* et al., *Social alcohol consumption and low Lp (2) lipoprotein concentration in middle aged Finnish men: population based study.* British Medical Journal, 316, *594, 1998: Barrett-Connor, E., and Suarez, L. A community study of alcohol and other factors associated with the distribution of high density lipoprotein cholesterol in older vs. younger men.* American Journal of Epidemiology, 115, *888, 1982: Willett, W., et al., Alcohol consumption and high density lipoprotein cholesterol in marathon runners.* New England Journal of Medicine, 303, *1159, 1980.*

[30] *Again there are numerous references. Langer, R.et al., Lipoprotein and blood pressure as biological pathways for effects of moderate alcohol consumption on coronary heart disease.* Circulation, 85 (3), *910, 1992: Castelli, W. P., et al., Alcohol and blood lipids. The cooperative lipoprotein phenotyping study.* The Lancet, 2, *153, 1977.*

[31] *Mukamal, K. J., et al., Alcohol consumption and lippoprotein subclasses in older adults.* Journal of Clinical Endocrinology & Metabolism, *2007 (April). PMID: 17440017.*

pressure. A possible outcome is that the heart becomes enlarged and the arteries are likely to be damaged.

What causes high blood pressure? In addition to age, obesity, and the excessive intake of salt, over-indulgence in alcohol is also well known to be a contributing factor to high blood pressure. The first scientist to describe the alcohol-blood pressure relationship was a French physician, Dr. Camille Lain. During the First World War, he monitored the blood pressures of soldiers who were moderate drinkers (up to 2 liters of wine a day), heavy drinkers (2 to 3 liters), and very heavy drinkers (over 3 liters). Lain found that the heaviest drinkers were more prone to high blood pressure, suggesting over consumption of alcohol may cause hypertension.

Since then there have been dozens of studies around the world addressing this issue, but the data are controversial. In 1977 Dr. Arthur Klatsky reported a U-shaped curve for the relationship between alcohol consumption and hypertension among women drinkers. The risk of high blood pressure was lower for women who were light-to-moderate drinkers, compared to those who either didn't drink at all or were heavy drinkers. Some studies in European countries also suggested that light drinking may significantly reduces blood pressure,[32] and also confirmed the positive benefits of alcohol use in reducing coronary artery disease.

2.2.4. Saké Protects Against Stroke

Stroke can seriously damage nerve cells in the brain and is often caused by an interrupted blood flow due to interference by a blood clot or due to the bursting of a blood vessel. Depending on the area of the brain affected, a stroke can cause coma, paralysis, speech problems and dementia. Strokes caused by clots that block the arteries are called ischemic strokes and account for 70 to 80 percent of all strokes. A second, less-common type of stroke is called a cerebral embolism, which involves a 'wandering' clot in the blood stream. It starts out elsewhere in the body, often in the heart, and makes its way to the brain.

The other types of stroke can be compared with the bursting of pipes carrying water in a residential dwelling with consequent flooding. These are called hemorrhagic strokes. Dozens of studies around world have been shown that a U-shaped curve describes the relationship between alcohol consumption and ischemic strokes; in other words, moderate drinking helps protect against ischemic stroke. That alcohol consumption in general reduces thrombosis or clot formation of blood has been reported. Mechanisms of reduction in platelet aggregation[33] in fibrinogen (a blood clotter) levels[34] as well as an increase in fibrinolysis (the dissolving of an already formed clot)[35] have been proposed

[32] *MacMahon, B., Alcohol consumption and hypertension.* Hypertension, *9 (2), 111, 1987; Dairdron, D. M., Cardiovascular effects of alcohol.* Western Journal of Medicine, 151 (4), *430, 1989.*

[33] *Meade, T. W., et al., Epidemiologic characteristics of platelet aggregability.* British Medical Journal, 290, *428, 1985; Jakubowshi, J. A.et al., Interaction of ethanol, prostacyclin, and aspirin in determining platelet reactivity in vitro.* Atherosclerosis, 8, *436, 1988.*

[34] *Wang, Z., and Barker, T., Alcohol at moderate levels decreases fibrinogen expression in vivo and in vitro.* Alcohol: Clinical and Experimental Research, 23, *1927, 1999.*

[35] *Sumi, H., et al., Urokinase-like plasminogen activator increased in plasma after alcohol drinking.*

In 1987 Dr. Ueshima et al. reported that people who drank saké moderately experienced a lower incidence of ischemic or clot-caused stroke compared to either non-drinkers or heavy drinkers. The U-shaped dependence found suggests moderate consumption of saké to be beneficial in preventing stroke. Free radicals are considered as the major species responsible for killing cells and tissue in our body. It is commonly generated as a by-product of normal metabolism but can also be sometimes induced by environmental factors, such as air pollution, solar ultraviolet radiation, ozone, and radioactive materials. It has been demonstrated that antioxidants present in saké (as well as in red wine) may play a major role in removing free radicals from body tissue and therefore help in preventing strokes.

2.3. Prevention of Coronary Artery Disease

The mortality rate due to coronary heart disease (CHD) is growing rapidly in Japan. Coronary artery disease (CAD) occurs when the arteries that supply blood to the heart (the coronary arteries) become hardened and narrowed due to build-up of a material called plaque on their inner walls. As the aterioscIerotic plaque increases in size, the lumen of the coronary arteries get narrower and less blood can flow through them. Eventually blood flow to the heart muscle is reduced to a point where it is not able to receive enough oxygen to function.

Reduced blood flow and oxygen supply to the heart muscle can result in chest pain and heart attacks.

Research has revealed an association between moderate alcohol consumption and lower risk for CHD. With few exceptions, dozens of epidemiologic studies from at least 20 countries in North America, Europe, and Asia, including Japan, demonstrate a 20-40 percent lower coronary heart disease (CHD) incidence among drinkers compared with nondrinkers. An example is the Harvard study[36] carried out in 1992. In this study moderate drinkers exhibited lower rates of CHD-related mortality than both heavy drinkers and abstainers. Such studies range from comparisons of nationwide population data to retrospective analyses of health and drinking patterns within large communities.

A National Institute on Alcohol Abuse and Alcoholism study[37] in 1996 found a cause-effect relationship between alcohol consumption in moderation and cardio protective benefits. The most persuasive epidemiologic evidence for alcohol's possible protective effects on CHD, however, comes from studies in which participants provided information on their drinking habits and health-related practices before the onset of CHD. In these studies the participants' subsequent health histories were evaluated through a series of follow up interviews.

The specific studies described here represent a total population of more than 1 million men and women of different ethnicities. The follow-up periods are on the

---

Alcohol & Alcoholism, 23, *33, 1988.*

[36] *Manson, J. E.,* et al., *The primary prevention of myocardial infarction.* The New England Journal of Medicine, 326 (21), *1406, 1992.*

[37] *Hennekens, C. H., Alcohol and Risk of Coronary Events. In: National Institute on Alcohol Abuse and Alcoholism.* Alcohol and the Cardiovascular System. *Washington, DC: U.S. Department of Health and Human Services (1996).*

average about 11 years; the longest was 24 years. The two largest studies confirming that moderate drinking can reduce the risk of CHD were conducted by the American Cancer Society, one including 276,800 men and the other including 490,000 men and women. A series of studies by Kaiser-Permanente analyzing CHD hospitalization and death rates in both men and women; studies of CHD incidence and mortality among female nurses; and studies of CHD incidence and mortality among male physicians, all agreed with this conclusion.

Results of these American studies are confirmed by data from similar investigations conducted in England, Denmark, China, and other countries. Medical evidence even goes so far as to draw the conclusion[38] that abstinence from alcohol is a major risk factor for coronary heart disease and that we have no drugs that are as good as alcohol in controlling CHD. [39] Not surprisingly, The American Heart Association, concluded[40] that the "consumption of one or two drinks per day is associated with a reduction in risk of (coronary heart disease) approximately 30% to 50%." The recommendation does not of course apply to those who are pregnant or about to get pregnant.

Even for the abstainers who do not benefit from the cardio-protective benefits, switching to moderate alcohol consumption after the first heart attack appears to be beneficial. Men who consume 2-4 drinks a day after a heart attack were 59% less likely than non-drinkers to have another heart attack.[41] The possibility of alcohol consumption reducing the damage to tissue after a heart attack has also been pointed out.[42]

However, the NIAA also warns that "If you can safely drink alcohol and you choose to drink, do so in moderation. Heavy drinking can actually increase the risk of heart failure, stroke, and high blood pressure, as well as cause many other medical problems, such as liver cirrhosis."

2.4. Taking Precautions against Diabetes Mellitus

Diabetes is a metabolic disease characterized by high blood glucose levels (hyperglycemia), resulting from either a diminished production of the hormone insulin in the body or physiological insensitivity to the hormone. Insulin, secreted by the pancreas, controls blood glucose levels in the body. Diabetes mellitus, commonly referred to as diabetes was first identified as a disease associated with "sweet urine," because of the excretion of glucose in the urine and was characterized by excessive muscle loss. Insulin is needed to convert sugar, starches and other food into the energy needed for daily life. Insulin lowers the blood glucose level. When the blood

---

[38] *Vin, sante & societe.* AIM, 4 (2), *7, 1995.*

[39] *Whitten, D., Wine Institute Seminar. San Francisco, CA: 1987. Quoted in Ford, G.* The French Paradox and Drinking for Health. *San Francisco, CA: Wine Appreciation Guild, p. 26 (1993).*

[40] *Pearson, Thomas A., (for the American Heart Association). Alcohol and heart disease.* Circulation, 94, *3023, 1996.*

[41] *de Lorgeril, M., et al., Wine drinking and risks of cardiovascular complications after recent acute myocardial infarction.* Circulation (American Heart Association), 106, *1465, 2002.*

[42] *Dayton C.et al., Antecedent ethanol prevents postischemic P-selection expression in murine small intestine.* Microcirculation, 11, *709, 2004.*

glucose elevates (for example, after eating a carbohydrate meal), insulin is released from the pancreas to normalize the glucose level. In patients with diabetes, however, the absence or insufficient production of insulin causes hyperglycemia. Diabetes can be controlled but is a chronic disease that lasts over a lifetime.

2.4.1. Diabetes, One of the Most Common Diseases in the World

In the United States alone, 20.8 million people currently suffer from diabetes. This means a whopping 7% of the population is coping with the disease. Every year thousands of people are diagnosed with diabetes in Japan, and with the ageing population this number is set to grow rapidly. Today 6.9 million children and adults suffer from the disease in Japan. It is predicted that, if current lifestyle habits remain unchanged, there will be 10.8 million people with diabetes by the year 2010. Unfortunately, many of these cases are more advanced than they need to be before they are diagnosed.

The longer a person suffers from diabetes the more difficult it is to revert the body back to its normal physiology. Therefore, it is imperative that the symptoms of diabetes be recognized early in order for the disease to be treated as soon as possible. Unfortunately, many of the minor symptoms of diabetes go unnoticed as the onset of this disease is so slow. If one has a family history of diabetes or exhibits any other diabetes risk factors, it is particularly important to be diligent about identifying the symptoms.

Studies agree that the chances of experiencing diabetes-related complications are significantly reduced the earlier the condition is treated. The risk increases with longer durations of the disease, poor blood glucose control, high blood pressure, and smoking. The most common complication of diabetes is damage of blood vessels in the heart, brain and legs (macrovascular complications), and damage to the small blood vessels, causing problems in the eyes, kidneys, feet and nerves (microvascular complications). Other parts of the body can also be affected by diabetes including the digestive system, skin and the immune system. Although this is not considered a related complication as such, people with diabetes may have higher incidence of thyroid problems than people without diabetes.

2.4.2. Saké Tends to Lower Blood Sugar

Dozens of studies have investigated the relationship between alcohol consumption and diabetes. Surprisingly, light to moderate drinkers of alcoholic beverages have a 30% to 40% lower diabetic risk than do abstainers. Recent research[43] suggests that consuming alcohol directly improves the action of insulin in patients with type 2 diabetes. The American Diabetes Association reports that "in people with diabetes, light-to-moderate amounts of alcohol are associated with a decreased risk of heart disease."

---

[43] *Carlsson, S., et al., Alcohol consumption and the incidence of type 2 diabetes: a 20-year follow-up of the Finnish Twin Cohort Study. Diabetes Care, 26 (10), 2785, 2003: Kopper, L., et al., Moderate alcohol consumption lowers the risk of type 2 diabetes: a meta-analysis of prospective observational studies. Diabetes Care, 28, 719, 2005.*

Another study reported that non-diabetic postmenopausal women can reduce insulin concentrations and improve insulin sensitivity by consuming alcohol in moderation. A major study of almost 21,000 physicians for over 12 years has found that men who are light to moderate drinkers have a decreased risk of type 2 diabetes. A study of 8,663 men over a period of as long as 25 years found that the incidence of type 2 diabetes was significantly lower among moderate drinkers than among either abstainers or heavy drinkers. A study of over 5,000 women with type 2 diabetes mellitus by Harvard researchers[44] also found that coronary heart disease (CHD) rates "were significantly lower in women who reported moderate alcohol intake than in those who reported drinking no alcohol."

Light to moderate consumption of alcohol also appears to reduce the risk of coronary heart disease by as much as 80% among individuals with older-onset diabetes, according to a study published in the Journal of the American Medical Association. Pre-menstrual women who consumed a daily drink of beer, wine or distilled spirits had a much lower risk of developing type 2 diabetes, compared to abstainers. Interestingly, light to moderate consumption of saké also appears to reduce blood sugar level, and therefore prevent diabetes, according to a study reported by Sato and Nakamura in 2003.

2.5. Prevention of Cancer

2.5.1. Alcohol and Cancer

Cancer is the leading cause of deaths in Japan, with one person out of three dying due to various forms of the disease. With the average age of the Japanese population increasing this problem will be exacerbated. Studies have shown that drinking alcohol, especially along with smoking, increases the risk of cancers of the mouth, esophagus, pharynx, larynx and liver in men, as well as of breast cancer in women. However, all these cancers are rare except for breast cancer.

The relationship between alcohol and breast cancer is unclear and remains controversial. Recent research[45] findings suggest that the intake of folate can offset any increased risk of breast cancer due to the consumption of alcohol. However, the moderate consumption of alcohol has not been associated with any of the common cancers except breast cancer.

In some instances, moderate consumption of alcohol was seen to reduce the risk of cancer. It is important to balance relative risks. Any increase in risk of an uncommon cancer needs to viewed in relation to the benefits of moderate drinking on reducing a major threat to health and contributing towards a long life. For example, about half of Americans die of heart attacks and moderate drinking reduces the risk of heart attacks by about 40%. Balancing such risks is a personal decision that should

---

[44] *Solomon, C. G., et al., Moderate alcohol consumption and risk of coronary heart disease among women with type 2 diabetes mellitus.* Circulation, 102, *494, 2000.*

[45] *Baglietto, L., et al., Does dietary folate intake modify effect of alcohol consumption on breast cancer risk? Prospective cohort study.* British Medical Journal, *August 8, 2005: Bailey, L.B. F., Methyl-related nutrients, alcohol and the MTHFR 677C -->T polymorphous affect cancer risk: Intake recommendations. Journal of Nutrition, 133, 37485, 2003.*

be discussed with one's physician. Although alcohol has both positive and negative effects, the benefits outweigh the risks for light-to-moderate drinkers.

Two well-designed cohort studies in Japan illustrate that moderate consumption of alcohol is not associated with most common forms of cancer. These also show that at least in some instances the consumption of saké reduced the risk of cancer. A cohort study, including xix prefectures, the so-called Hirayama's Cohort Study, evaluated the relationship between cancer risk and life style. This study, carried out over 1965-1982, included 265,118 people aged 40 years or above (122,261 men and 142,857 women). The cancer risks were found to be lower for Japanese with Seventh-Day Adventists (SDA) life-styles, i.e., no smoking, no drinking, no meat consumption daily, and eating green and yellow vegetables daily. One surprising result from this study is that in the SDA population, moderate consumption of alcohol further reduced the risk of the most common cancers significantly, as shown in Figure 8.

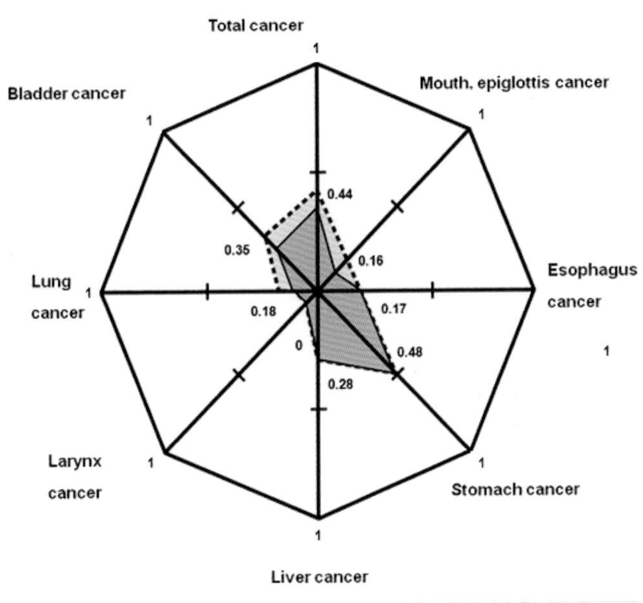

(From Hirayama, T., et al, 1977)

Figure 8: A radar diagram illustrating the decrease in cancer associated with moderate consumption of alcohol in Japanese adult vegetarian population.

Saké consumption reduces the risk of the most common cancers significantly. The cancer risks of the enclosure by oblique lines agree well with the risk which shows the one by oblique line (life-stylists: no smoking, no drinking, no meat consumption daily and eating green and yellow vegetables daily).

Interestingly, as shown in Figure 9, the risks of cancers of the lungs, liver, and the gastrointestinal were much less in men aged 40-54 years who were moderate consumers of alcohol, compared to abstainers. This data differs from findings in

Western countries; possibly due the fact that most of the alcohol consumed in Japan is saké.

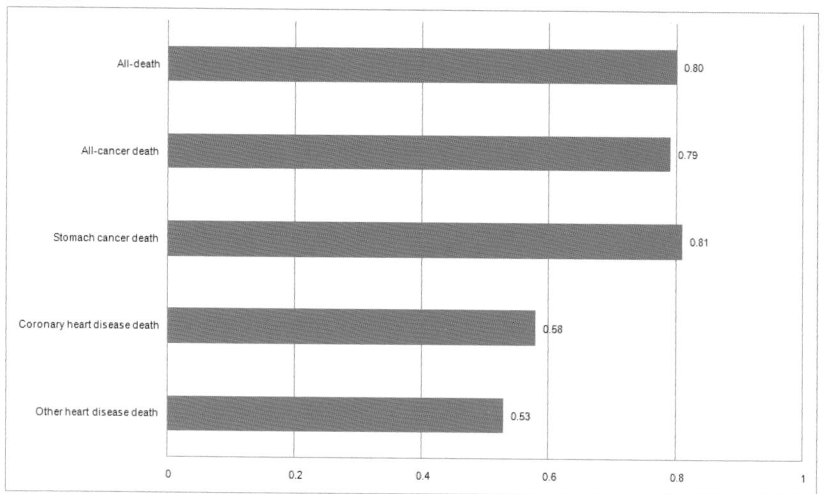

(From Hirayama, T., 1994)

The overall of death was found to be decreased in drinkers. Sex-specific and aged-adjusted hazard ratios were calculated.

Figure 9: The relative risk of those who consume moderate amounts of saké daily. The corresponding risk for non-drinkers is set at 1.0.

A second pertinent study is the Japan Collaborative Cohort Study for Evaluation of Cancer Risk (JACC Study), a large prospective cohort study, which was carried out from 1988 to 1990 in 45 areas in Japan. It included 110,792 (46,465 men and 64,327 women) 40-79 years of age at the time of the base line survey. During an average follow-up period of 8 years (up to 1987) Ohno et al. documented 3,458 incidents of cancers. Cancer-related deaths accounted for 39.2% of the deaths in men and 37.9% in the women. Table 1 shows the relative risk of various cancers correlated with alcohol consumption. The age-adjusted relative risk for regular drinkers was significantly lower for all-cancer deaths, liver cancers, gallbladder/bile duct cancers, stomach cancers and lung cancers, compared with that for abstainers. However, the risk for heavy drinkers was significantly higher. A U-shaped relationship was found between alcohol consumption and the risk of death by cancer (Ohno, Y., et al., 2002).

Cause of cancer death	Drinkers	Stop-drinkers	Non-drinkers
Total mortality	0.85	1.77	
Total cancer	0.89	1.55	
Mouth,epiglottis cancer	1.29	1.79	
Esophagus cancer	2.55	3.08	
Stomach cancer	0.87	1.43	-1.00-
Colon cancer	1.07	1.31	
Rectum cancer	0.87	1.77	
Liver cancer	0.83	3.64	
Gall bladder cancer	0.77	1.81	

(From Ohono, Y. et al.,1995.)

Table 1: Difference in mortality from different types of cancer in regular saké drinkers compared to that for those who stopped regular intake of saké.

Studies have clearly demonstrated the beneficial effects of alcohol intake on at least two types of cancer. Analysis of a set of 12 prospective studies involving over 750,000 subjects found that moderate drinkers enjoy a 30% lower risk of kidney cancer relative to abstainers.[46] For women the advantage might be even greater; a 66% lower risk was reported in a Scandinavian study.[47] The same was true also of Non-Hodgkin's Lymphoma, with the risk of developing the cancer lower by 27% for moderate drinkers (compared to abstainers).[48] While not fully established in repeated well-controlled studies, there are indications that moderate drinking may protect against several other forms of cancer as well (colorectal cancer[49], endometrial cancer and thyroid cancer in women.[50])

2.5.2. Saké Inhibits Tumor Cellular Growth

Unlike other types of alcohol, saké contains a range of more than 120 nutrients, such as amino acids, organic acids, sugar, and vitamins. More than ten years ago, Dr. Takizawa's group reported that saké concentrate inhibited the growth by up to 90 percent in cancer cells derived from bladder cancer, prostate cancer, and uterus cancer tissue. The saké concentrate did not inhibit the growth of these cells in a dose-dependent manner, but the inhibition was still evident at very low concentrations of the saké concentrate. As shown in Figure 10, the growth rate of bladder cancer

[46] *Lee, J. E., et al., Alcohol intake and renal cell cancer in a pooled analysis of 12 prospective studies. Journal of the National Cancer Institute, 99, 811, 2007.*

[47] *Rashidkhani, B., et al., Alcohol consumption and risk of renal cell carcinoma: A prospective study of Swedish women. International Journal of Cancer, 117 (5), 848, 2005.*

[48] *Morton, L., et al., Alcohol consumption and risk of non-Hodgkin lymphoma: A pooled analysis Lancet Oncology, June 8, 2005.*

[49] *Austin, Gregory.et al., Moderate Alcohol Consumption Protects Against Colorectal Adenoma. Paper presented at Digestive Diseases Week (DDW), May 24, 2006, abstract M2263.*

[50] *Rossing, M. A., et al., Risk of papillary thyroid cancer in women in relation to smoking and alcohol consumption.* Epidemiology, 11, *49, 2000.*

cells treated with saké concentrate was particularly slow, and eventually most cells were killed. Significantly, this inhibitory effect of saké on cancer cells was only seen with saké, but not with distilled spirits such as whisky or brandy.

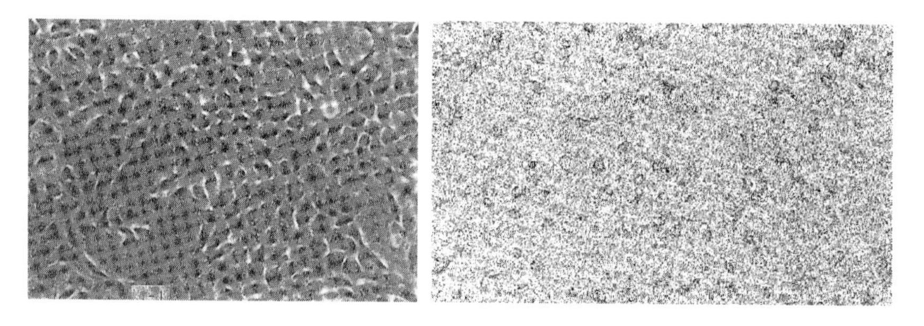

Bladder cancer cells (Control) | Bladder cancer cells after saké-concentrator treatment

(From Takizawa, Y. et al., 1994)

Figure 10: Apoptosis of cancer cells in vitro on treatment with saké concentrate.

The human cells originated in bladder-transitional epithelial cancer (Japan Cell Bank). The control cells showed typical growth on day 5. In contrast, the cells treated with the Sake sample showed a cytopathogenic effect image with voids among cells due to the concentration of the surviving cells and the peeling off the necrotic cells.

2.5.3. Breast Cancer in Women

The incidence of breast cancer among Japanese women, a traditionally low-risk population, has increased dramatically in recent years and has become the most common form of cancer in women. An estimated 34,000 cases occurred in 1998, and this accounted for 15.8% of all new cases of cancer. Both genetic and environmental factors play an important role in the development of breast cancer. Most studies have shown a modestly increased risk of breast cancer with alcohol consumption although the results are still controversial.

However, according to research at the Centre for Alcohol Research at the National Institute for Public Health in Denmark, moderate drinking of alcoholic beverages appears to have little effect on women's risk of developing breast cancer,. New data from the ongoing Framingham study also indicate that moderate consumption of alcohol does not increase the risk of breast cancer. A study on 17,000 women found that those who consume about three drinks per day, but take 200 micrograms of folic acid (Vitamin B9) per day, have a lower risk of breast cancer than do alcohol abstainers. Folic acid appears to offset the risk of breast cancer in women who drink in moderation.

Consumption of wine, especially red wine, has recently become popular due to its relatively high concentration of polyphenols (mostly flavanoids and resveratrol). Polyphenolic compounds have antioxidant activities and are therefore thought to function well as anti-carcinogens. A number of studies have demonstrated the chemopreventive action of resveratrol against cancer. Resveratrol has been shown to significantly lower tumor growth, decrease blood vessel formation, and decrease breast cancer cell survival in resveratrol-treated nude mice compared with control animals. Resveratrol naturally occurs in grapes and is therefore found in red wine.

Resveratrol at high concentrations suppresses breast cancer cell growth in all the tested breast-cell lines. This suppression was due to apoptosis, an active process requiring metabolic activity by the dying cell. Thus, resveratrol could be a promising anticancer agent for breast cancers, and may mitigate the growth stimulatory effect of linoleic acid in the Western-style diet.

2.5.4. *Prostate Cancer*

Prostate cancer is a leading cause of cancer deaths among Japanese men. Although age, ethnic origin and a positive family history of prostate cancer have been established as important risk factors, its etiology remains largely unknown. Environmental and other factors suspected to be associated with increased risk of prostate cancer include poor diet, occupation, smoking, sexual and physical activity, hormonal levels (androgens and estrogens), and body size.

A well-designed study was conducted by Dr. Stanford at the University of Washington, which investigated the relationship between alcohol consumption and prostate cancer. A total of 753 newly diagnosed prostate cancer cases, 40-64 years of age, as well as 703 control subjects (matched to the test cases by age) participated in the study. All participants completed an in-person interview on lifetime alcohol consumption and other risk factors for prostate cancer. The findings suggest that the consumption of red wine may be associated with a reduction in the risk of prostate cancer, especially the more aggressive forms of cancer. Each additional glass of red wine consumed per week showed further significant decrease in the relative risk of prostate cancer.

These findings offer a new perspective on the possible role of alcohol consumption in relation to prostate cancer and highlight the need for further research on the biological effects of polyphenol-rich foods and beverages.

Benign enlargement of the prostate is a condition that affects more than half of men over the age of approximately 50. Although hyperplasia is benign it is still a difficult condition to live with. Consuming two or more alcoholic drinks per day has been reported[51] to reduce the risk of this disease by 33%.

2.6. Prevention of Liver Disease

Liver disease (cirrhosis) is one of the most common of modern diseases and the incidence of this disease has also increased in Japan over the recent years. It is reported that more than 2,000,000 and 200,000 people currently suffer from chronic hepatitis and cirrhosis of the liver respectively in Japan. Usually, individuals at risk for

---

[51] *Kristal, A. R. A., et al., Dietary Patterns, Supplement Use, and the Risk of Symptomatic Benign Prostatic Hyperplasia: Results from the Prostate Cancer Prevention Trial.* American Journal of Epidemiology, *February 2, 2008.*

developing liver cancer are those already suffering from cirrhosis. In other words, cirrhosis appears to be a precancerous condition. Those with cirrhosis from chronic hepatitis C, chronic hepatitis B, hemochromatosis, excessive consumption of alcohol, or a fatty liver, are at increased risk of developing liver cancer.

It is genially accepted that over-consumption of alcohol can damage the liver. Alcohol-induced liver disease is common, but preventable. Its severity depends on how long a person has been consuming alcohol. There are three primary types of alcohol-induced liver diseases:

Fatty liver: Fatty liver is an excessive accumulation of fat inside the liver cells. It is the most common alcohol-induced liver disorder. The liver is enlarged, causing upper abdominal discomfort on the right side.

Alcoholic hepatitis: Alcoholic hepatitis is an acute inflammation of the liver, accompanied by the destruction of individual liver cells and scarring of the tissue. Symptoms may include fever, jaundice, an increased white blood cell count, an enlarged, tender liver, and spider-like veins in the skin.

Alcoholic cirrhosis: Alcoholic cirrhosis is the destruction of normal liver tissue, leaving behind only the non-functioning scar tissue. Symptoms may include those of alcoholic hepatitis, in addition to portal hypertension, enlarged spleen, kidney failure, or liver cancer.

Epidemiologic evidence indicates the mortality rate from cirrhosis to be directly related to the per capita consumption of alcohol from wine and spirits. The age-standardized mortality ratio (SMR) for liver cirrhosis and liver cancer for the period of 1969 to 1978 in the 46 prefectures are given in Figure 11. As can be seen, the developmental SMRs of these diseases vary in different localities. The highest mortalities appear to be in the west and the lowest in the east of Japan.

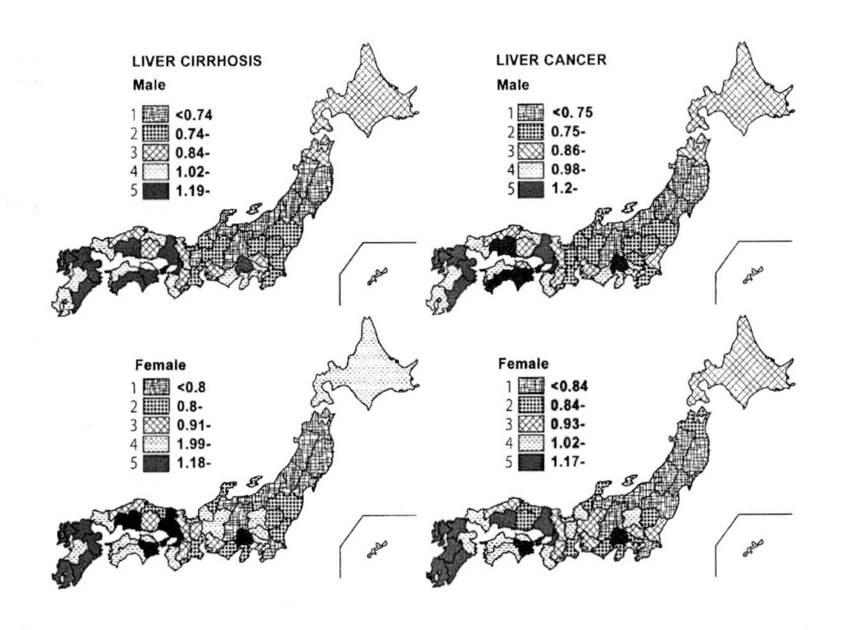

(From Takizawa, Y. et al., 1985)

Figure 11: Age-standardized mortality due to cirrhosis and liver cancer in Japan during 1969-1978.

In order to assess the profile for this condition better, Dr. Takizawa analyzed the data first from the standpoint of the types of alcohol consumed, then evaluated other risk factors. The results from his study indicated that saké consumption was negatively correlated with liver cirrhosis at a statistically significant level. The correlations, however, were positive for whiskey, brandy, *shochu* and beer. This is a surprising result given that it is the alcohol that is believed to cause liver disease. Although alcohol consumption in Japanese is relatively high, mortality due to liver cirrhosis is low in Japan compared to rest of the world. This result suggests that any benefits (in preventing cirrhosis) associated with consuming saké, cannot be extended to other types of alcoholic beverages.

One of the major functions of the liver is to synthesize protein from amino acids that are required our normal life. In those suffering from cirrhosis of the liver, protein synthesis is impaired due to the lack of some important amino acids such as leucine, isoleucine, and valine. Saké, as mentioned, contains all three of these amino acids as well as numerous others, suggesting moderate consumption of saké may supply the lacking amino acids. In fact a common treatment option for alcohol-induced liver disease is supplementation of specific amino acids to restore some or all of the normal functioning to the liver. The liver is naturally endowed with great restorative power and is often able to repair some of the damage caused by alcohol. In most cases, the only damage it cannot reverse is scarring from cirrhosis.

In 1984, Dr. Takizawa group conducted a well-designed study to investigate the relationship between liver diseases and saké consumption across the Japan. As shown in Table 2, saké consumption was found to be significantly negatively correlated with the incidence of liver cirrhosis. The correlation was, however, significantly positive for whiskey, brandy, shochu and beer. This conclusion is consistent with the previous report from Drs. Shigematsu and Matsushita (1962), which indicated that saké, but not other types of alcohol, decreased the incidence of liver cirrhosis. The epidemiologic evidence indicates that the contribution of alcohol to the incidence of liver cirrhosis is very different in Japanese populations and those in Western countries. In Western countries, the association between alcohol and liver cirrhosis accounts for 60-80 percent of the cases, but the study conducted by Dr. Suzuki (1993) demonstrated that the contribution of alcohol to liver cirrhosis only accounts for only 20-30 percent of the cases in Japan.

Type of sake	Male	Female
Sake	-0.427**	-0.400**
Beer	0.282	0.327
Whisky	0.203	0.151
Shochu	0.342*	0.324*
Au antigen positive	**0.342***	**0.380***

(From Takizawa, Y., et al., 1984)

These differences are highly significant; *at P<0.05 and **at P<0.01.

Table 2: Age-standardized mortality due to cirrhosis of the liver in adults who consumed different types of alcohol on a regular basis.

2.7. Osteoporosis and Saké

Osteoporosis is a disease in which the bones become fragile, more likely to break, and heal slowly after damage. These broken bones, also known as fractures, occur typically in the hip, spine, and wrist. It is largely caused by loss of calcium and other mineral components, sometimes resulting in pain, decreased height, and skeletal deformities. It is characterized by low bone mass and structural deterioration of the bone that often develops increased porosity. Osteoporosis is more common in older persons, primarily postmenopausal women, but is also associated with long-term steroid therapy and certain endocrine disorders. Any bone can be affected, but hip fractures are relatively common, and usually require hospitalization and major surgery. It can impair a person's ability to walk unassisted and may cause prolonged or permanent disability and in some cases even death.

Osteoporosis is a major public health threat in Japan. One in two women and one in four men over age 50 will have an osteoporosis-related fracture in her or his remaining lifetime. Osteoporosis is often called a "silent disease" because the bone deterioration occurs slowly and without obvious or typical symptoms. People may not know that they have osteoporosis until their bones become so weak that a sudden strain, bump or fall causes a fracture or a vertebra to collapse. Collapsed vertebrae may initially be felt or seen in the form of severe back pain, loss of height, or spinal deformities. Although there is no cure for osteoporosis it is preventable.

By about the age 20, the average woman has acquired 98 percent of her skeletal mass. Building strong bones during childhood and adolescence can be the best defense against developing osteoporosis later in life. Many steps can be taken to maintain good bone health and help prevent osteoporosis. Among them, the most important is to take well-balanced diet rich in calcium and vitamin D, as well as to engage in regular weight-bearing and resistance-training exercises.

Several studies have shown moderate alcohol consumption to have beneficial effects in preventing osteoporosis. Dr. Hoidrup et al., Denmark, studied the association between quantity and type of alcohol intake and risk of hip fracture among 17,868 men and 13,917 women. Analyses were based on pooled data from three population studies conducted in 1964-1992 in Copenhagen, Denmark. The risk of hip fracture differed according to the type of alcohol the subjects consumed: beer had a higher risk of hip fracture than other types of alcoholic beverages. The corresponding relative risks for wine and spirits were 0.77 and 0.82, respectively. Their results suggest that an alcohol intake within the current European drinking limits does not influence the risk of hip fracture, whereas an alcohol intake of more than 27 drinks per week is a major risk factor for men.

Dr. Van Thiel et al., University of Pittsburgh, USA, examined the relationship between serum estradiol and moderate alcohol consumption in a group of 128 osteoporosis patients. Estradiol levels were found to be significantly increased in alcohol users as compared to abstainers, and estradiol levels were significantly correlated with total weekly drinks consumed. They concluded that the increase in estradiol levels seen with moderate alcoholic beverage consumption was not an isolated finding and speculated that moderate alcohol consumption by healthy postmenopausal women may have beneficial effects.

Dr. Hobrook et al., of the University of California, San Diego, conducted a study to investigate the effects of alcohol consumption on bone mineral density in a defined population, measuring and monitoring their bone mineral density during 1988-91. Their data demonstrate that with increasing alcohol intake, bone mineral density increased significantly in both men and women, and they concluded that social drinking was associated with higher bone mineral density in men and women.

2.8. Prevention of Senile Dementia

2.8.1. What is Dementia?

Dementia is a neurological disorder that affects one's ability to think, speak, reason, remember and move. While Alzheimer's disease is the most typical and common cause of dementia, many other conditions can also cause similar symptoms. Some of these disorders get worse with time and cannot be completely cured. Other types of the condition respond so well to treatment that their symptoms may even be reversed.

After Alzheimer's disease, the most common forms of dementia are vascular dementia and Lewy body dementia. Sometimes, a person can have more than one of these conditions at the same time. In vascular dementia, arteries feeding the brain become narrowed or blocked. The onset of symptoms usually is abrupt, frequently occurring after a stroke. However, some forms of vascular dementia progress so slowly that they are difficult to distinguish from Alzheimer's disease. Some people have both Alzheimer's and vascular dementia at the same time. Vascular dementia often causes problems with thinking ability, language, walking, bladder control and vision. Preventing additional strokes by treating underlying diseases, such as high blood pressure, may halt the progression of vascular dementia. Because it affects areas of the brain that are responsible for judgment and social behavior, front temporal dementia can result in socially inappropriate behavior. Symptoms of this form of dementia, which runs in families, usually appear between the ages of 40 and 65.

Dementia rates appeared to be low in Japan initially, but the numbers of dementia cases increases each year due to an increase in the elderly population. It is now a major public health threat for an estimated 1.6 million elderly people with dementia in 2000. This increase has come about as a by-product of a widely shared material prosperity, resulting in a life-expectancy that is about the highest in the world. Japan used to have a traditional value system that accorded high status to the elderly. However in reality, three-generational living has declined dramatically in recent years. Support of aged parents by their children can no longer to be taken for granted in Japan. Many old people with dementia are isolated and neglected in the countryside, without appropriate health care from either the public or their children.

2.8.2. Light-to-moderate Drinking Reduces Risk of Dementia

Alcohol consumption has been associated with complex changes in cerebral vasculature and structure in older people. Many studies have been conducted to explore how alcohol consumption affects the incidence of dementia. Dr. Ruitenberg et al. in the Netherlands conducted a study based on the hypothesis that alcohol consumption might affect the risk of dementia. They examined the relation between alcohol consumption and the risk of dementia in individuals taking part in the Rotterdam Study, a prospective population-based study of 7983 individuals aged 55 years and older. They studied all participants who did not have dementia at baseline (1990-93) and who had complete data on their alcohol consumption (n=5395). Through follow-up examinations in 1993-94 and 1997-99 and an extensive monitoring system, they obtained nearly complete follow-up (99.7%) until the end of 1999.

The risk of developing dementia in individuals who regularly consumed alcohol and those who did not consume alcohol was recorded. The average follow-up period was 6 years, and 197 individuals developed dementia (146 Alzheimer's disease, 29 vascular dementia, 22 other dementia). The median alcohol consumption was 0.29 drinks per day. Light-to-moderate drinking (one to three drinks per day) was significantly associated with a lower risk of any dementia and also for vascular dementia. They found no evidence that the relation between alcohol and dementia varied by the type of alcoholic beverage consumed. These findings suggest that light-to-moderate alcohol consumption is associated with a reduced risk of dementia in individuals aged 55 years or older.

Other studies agree with the above conclusion. A US study based on 6,000 people for instance, found moderate consumption of alcohol to reduce the incidence of dementia by 54% compared to abstainers.[52] Patients suffering from mild cognitive impairment, sometimes progress into dementia. Recent studies [53] show that consuming a drink of alcohol a day, and even less, may slow this process down.

Vascular dementia is more common than Alzheimer's disease in Japan, while Alzheimer's disease is much more frequent in Western countries. The Hisayama study, an epidemiological study on dementia in a Japanese elderly population aged 65 years or older, has shown that the risk factors for vascular dementia were age, hypertension, previous stroke, and alcohol consumption, while age was only a significant risk factor for Alzheimer's disease. Comparison between alcohol consumption and the risk of dementia in Japan has shown light-to-moderate drinking significantly reduces the risk of Alzheimer's disease as well as vascular dementia in individuals aged 55 years or older. The negative association between moderate drinking of saké and cardiovascular morbidity is well documented. Saké also has a beneficial effect on senile dementia.

Alcohol consumption has not been recognized as a risk factor in previous epidemiologic studies. Dr. Orgogozo et al., at Bordeaux University, France, prospectively studied 3,800 individuals aged 65 and over. Incidence of dementia and Alzheimer's disease were screened at follow-up interviews using explicit criteria. At 3 years, 2,273 subjects not demented at baseline were still available for follow-up. Their result indicates that people over 65 who drink wine moderately have a significantly lower risk of vascular dementia and Alzheimer's disease.

Dr. Mukamal et al., of Beth Israel Deaconess Medical Center, Boston, investigated the relationship of alcohol consumption and risk of dementia among older adults. Nested case-control study of 373 cases with incident dementia and 373 controls who were among 5,888 adults aged 65 years and older who participated in the Cardiovascular Health Study (a prospective, population-based cohort study in 4 US communities) was used. Odds of incident dementia, ascertained by detailed neurological and neuropsychological examinations were compared to self-reported average alcohol consumption of beer, wine, and liquor at 2 visits prior to the date of the magnetic resonance imaging (MRI). Compared with abstention, the adjusted odds for dementia among those whose weekly alcohol consumption was less than 1 drink were 0.65; 1 to 6 drinks, 0.46; 7 to 13 drinks, 0.69; and 14 or more drinks, 1.22. A trend toward greater odds of dementia associated with heavier alcohol consumption was most apparent among men. They found generally similar relationships of alcohol use with Alzheimer disease and vascular dementia. The conclusion from this study is that compared with abstention, consumption of 1 to 6 drinks weekly is associated with a lower risk of incident dementia among older adults.

[52] *Mulkamal, K. J., et al., Prospective study of alcohol consumption and risk of dementia in older adults. Journal of the American Medical Association, 289, 1405, 2003.*

[53] *American Academy of Neurology. A Drink a Day May Delay Dementia. Press release, May 21 (2007); Solfrizzi, Vencenzo et al., Alcohol consumption, mild cognitive impairment, and progression to dementia. Neurology, 68 (2), 2007.*

2.8.3. Peptides in Saké Improves the Capacity of Memory

A hormone called vasopressin plays an important role in the capacity for memory and learning. Vasopressin is secreted by the posterior pituitary gland and also by nerve endings in the hypothalamus. Vasopressin also affects blood pressure by stimulating capillary muscles and reduces urine flow. It is known that memory impediment or deterioration of learning occurs when vasopressin is inhibited or depleted. Vasopressin activity is largely controlled by inhibitors such as prolyl endopeptidase (PEP), which exists in our brain and cuts off the vasopressin peptide bond at the carboxyl site of proline residue. In other words, the capacity of memory and learning is impaired when excess PEP inactivates bioactive vasopressin. Indeed, it was confirmed that the PEP activity of dementia patients was very high and vasopressin in these patients was unusually decomposed. It is expected that the prevention or treatment of dementia may be possible by inhibition of PEP.

Recently, Kawato et al., of the Research Institute, Gekkeikan Saké Co., Ltd purified and identified several peptides from saké and its byproduct saké remains. These peptides function as potent inhibitors of PEP, and therefore increase the ability and capacity of memory and learning. They also reported that systolic blood pressure decreased significantly when these peptides were orally administered to spontaneously hypertensive rats. Dr. Yoshimoto et al., also reported that these PEP inhibitors purified from saké and its byproduct saké remains significantly improved animals' memories when these inhibitors were orally administered to animals.

A recent study carried out in New Zealand[54] also agrees that moderate drinking can improve short-term memory. Working with the rat model the researchers concluded that alcohol intake may contribute to cognition and memory by directly acting on the brain (via adaptive changes in hippocampal NMDA receptor expression).

2.9. What is Moderate Drinking?

As discussed in the previous sections of this chapter a body of well-documented research from all over the world suggests that moderate consumption of alcoholic beverages (such as Japanese saké) can prevent a host of different diseases. The critical question here is how much alcohol is a moderate amount? Definitions of moderate drinking vary among studies. The U.S. Department of Agriculture and the U.S. Department of Health and Human Services define moderate drinking as not more than two drinks per day for men and no more than one drink per day for women. A standard drink is 12 grams of pure alcohol, which is equivalent to one 12-ounce bottle of beer, one 5-ounce glass of wine, or 1.5 ounces of distilled spirits. Harvard researchers concluded[55] that the consumption of one or two drinks of beer, wine, or liquor per day corresponded to a reduction in risk of coronary heart disease by approximately 20-40%. Each of these contain approximately 0.6

---

[54] *Kalev-Zylinska, M. L. and During, M. J., Paradoxical facilitatory effect of low-dose alcohol consumption on memory mediated by NMDA receptors.* Journal of Neuroscience, *27, 10456, 2007.*

[55] *Manson, J. E., et al.,* Prevention of Myocardial Infarction. *New York: Oxford University Press (1996).*

ounces of alcohol, but the portion of beer has about 50% more calories than the wine or the spirits,

A study of 18,455 males from the Physicians Health Study[56] revealed that those originally consuming only a single drink or less per week, but who increased their consumption to six drinks per week, found a 29% reduction in Cardio Vascular Disease (CVD) risk compared to those who did not increase their consumption. Men originally consuming 1-6 drinks per week who increased their consumption moderately had a 15% decrease in CVD risk compared to those who made no change. It is, however, not clear at what point the increased protection afforded by increased consumption tapers off or stops. However, it should be abundantly clear that drinking a week's worth of 6-12 drinks on a single day and abstaining the rest of the week has no preventative value and is likely to result in serious health problems. Heavy drinking is associated with early mortality and increased risk factors for a large number of diseases.

A large body of research literature supports the position that moderate intake of alcohol either as a brewed beverage or as a distilled spirit prevents the incidence of many serious diseases. The space here does not permit the referencing and a description of all the relevant research. The author will therefore list here for the benefit of the readers those medical conditions where some benefit of alcohol intake in reducing its incidence has been clearly documented:

Cardiovascular diseases, stroke, hypertension, siabetes, Alzheimer's disease or Dementia, common cold, kidney cancer, metabolic syndrome, Non-Hodgkin's lymphoma, peripheral artery disease, Angina Pectoris, bone fractures and osteoporosis, digestive ailments, duodenal ulcer, erectile dysfunction, essential tremors, gallstones, hearing loss, Hepatitis A, Hodgkin's Lymphoma (cancer), kidney stones, macular degeneration (a major cause of blindness), pancreatic cancer, Parkinson's disease, poor cognition and memory, poor physical condition in elderly, stress and depression, Type B Gastritis, Rheumatoid arthritis (Hanson 2008).

2.10. References Regarding the Health Benefits of Saké

Pearl, R., Alcohol and Longevity New York: Alfred A. Knopf, p.273, 1926.

Maskarinec, G., et al., Alcohol intake, body weight, and mortality in a multiethnic prospective cohort. Epidemiology, 9, 654, 1998.

Gaziano, J. M., et al., Light-to-moderate alcohol consumption and mortality in the Physicians' Health Study enrollment cohort. Journal of the American College of Cardiology, 35, 96, 2000.

Farchi, G., et al., Alcohol and survival in the Italian rural cohorts of the Seven countries Study. International Journal of Epidemiology, 29, 667, 2000.

---

[56] *Sesso, H. D.,* et al., *Seven -year changes in alcohol consumption and subsequent risk of cardiovascular disease in men.* Archives of Internal Medicine, 160, *2505, 2001.*

Maraldi, C., et al., Impact of inflammation on the relationship among alcohol consumption, mortality, and cardiac events: the Health, Aging, and Body Composition Study. Archives of Internal Medicine, 166, 1490, 2006.

McCallum, J., et al., The Dubbo Study of the Health of the Elderly 1988-2002: An Epidemiological Study of Hospital and Residential Care. Sydney, NSW, Australia: The Australian Health Policy Institute (2003).

Hanson, D. J. (2008)
http://www2.potsdam.edu/hansondj/Controversies/1088441583.html

Chapter 3: Learning About Saké, Japan's National Beverage

3.1. A Brief History of Saké

Saké has maintained a prominent presence in Japanese life and culture for thousands of years. Today its popularity continues to grow, expanding even beyond the boundaries of Japan to reach other parts of the world. While the exact beginnings of this exotic beverage is not clear, the practice of brewing rice wine is believed to have originated along the Yangtze river in ancient China (in the Yunnan and Guizhou provinces)[57] about 4,000 years ago.

The knowledge of saké-making probably followed the same distribution routes of rice itself, first into the neighboring provinces and then into countries in Asia. The first description of Japanese saké (*nihonshu*) dates back to approximately 3,000 BCE, to the middle of the Jomon period. Consuming saké as well as making an offering of it to deities was a harvest ritual in Japan at the time. Another theory suggests that the Japanese started producing saké about the same time the cultivation of wet rice started in the third century BCE. Regardless of the exact origins of saké-brewing, the Japanese are widely credited with mass production and refinement of the beverage.

Having enjoyed a long history as the only alcoholic beverage available, the popularity of saké in Japan is not surprising. Its health benefits were recognized early in the history of saké. In addition to being a sought-after beverage, saké also played an important role in the Japanese culture and religion. It was used in Shinto religious practices to purify temples and also as an offering to deities, leading to saké-brewing being taken up even by the priests (*souboushu*). In Shinto wedding ceremonies the bride and groom each consumed saké in a traditional practice known as *sansankudo*.

3.1.1. The Early Years of Saké

The very first varieties of saké were called *kuchikami-no-saké*, meaning "chewed-in-the-mouth sake," because to prepare the grain for fermentation the early saké–makers chewed the rice grains and spit out the chewed rice into a container. This chewing process polished the rice to some extent, ground it and mixed the rice-starch with saliva. Salivary amylase enzymes were able to convert the starch into sugar that could then be fermented into alcohol. This watery mixture was combined with freshly-cooked grain and allowed to naturally ferment into saké. This very primitive means of manufacture changed with discovery of *koji*, the mold Aspergillus oryzae used in the manufacture of saké.

The origins of consistent manufacturing practices for Japanese saké emerged probably in the Heian era (794 CE-1185 CE). As the process improvements in saké-making came about mainly by trial and error, the competing small breweries jealously guarded the details of their processes. Experimentation by Japanese

---

[57] *Interestingly this region in China is reported to no longer produce saké, but only distilled spirits [Lisdiyanti, P. & Kozakai, M., Proceedings of 1st International Symposium on Insight into the World of Indegenous Fermented Foods for Technology Development and Food Safety. pp. I-3 Bangkok, Thailand (2003).*

brewers and the introduction of more recent brewing techniques from China sometime in the 7th century CE, helped further improve the quality of saké.[58] Centuries later, a yeast mash or *shubo*, was discovered as a key additive to convert the sugars to ethanol. This was an important development that potentially increased the alcohol content in saké (to 18%-22% by volume).

The first varieties of Japanese saké were likely produced by non-professional individual brewers, farming families or even by small villages. The largest production area in early Japan was centered around Nada, near the city of Kobe. Although saké was manufactured on a relatively modest scale at the time, it appears to have been consumed only by the upper classes or the nobility. By then brewers were already producing different varieties of saké for consumption by different social classes or ranks of the nobility. It was only during the Kamakura and Muromachi periods (1100 CE-1500 CE) did saké become accepted as a popular beverage to be enjoyed by the masses. Serious mass production of saké began in the 14th century when it was produced commercially in small breweries set in the countryside, for public consumption on market days.[59]

The three-step process including the addition of ingredients in the brewing process was developed in the Heian Era (794 CE-1185 CE). This technique increases the alcohol content and reduces the chances of souring of the beverage. By that period, saké had gained favor in the imperial palace and an official department to promote and regulate its manufacture was instituted. This resulted for the first time in recognizing professional 'brew masters,' or full-time saké brewers. It is these dedicated craftsmen who paved the way to many future improvements and fine-tuning of the manufacturing technique.

Research suggests that by the 14th century saké had become a common drink to be enjoyed by all and it was freely available in public events such as market days.[2,3] (Smith 1992 149; Kondo 1996 21). By the Tokugawa period mass celebrations and public feasting routinely included the consuming of saké. For the next 500 years, the brewing techniques and consequently the quality of saké, dramatically improved. The basic brewing technology and the basics of mechanization of the process can be traced back to this very active period in the history of saké. For instance, the use of *moto*, a starter mash to cultivate the maximum concentration of yeast cells to initiate fermentation, came into use at this time. Brewers were also able to isolate *koji* for the first time, and thus they were able to control with some consistency the saccharification (converting starch to sugar) of the rice.

With this popularization of saké it also became easier for individuals and families to set up small breweries in Japan. During the Meiji Restoration, laws were written to allow anyone who had the knowledge to build their own saké brewery. Nearly 30,000 breweries sprang up all around the country within a few years. Saké from different regions of the country evolved their distinct identities based on their

---

[58] *Kondo, H., Saké: A Drinker's Guide. Tokyo New York, London: Kodansha International Ltd. (1966)*

[59] *Smith, S., "Drinking Etiquette in a Changing beverage Market". In "Re-made in Japan: Everyday Life and Consumer Taste in Changing Society." ED: J. Tobin. Yale University Press, New Haven (1992).*

unique aroma and taste.[60] In addition to the smaller home-based breweries, large commercial operations also prospered during this period.

As the years passed, however, the government gradually increased the taxes it levied on saké breweries, eventually shrinking their numbers down to about 8,000. Most of the owners who managed to survive this difficult period eventually became wealthy owners of breweries. The most successful of these family-owned breweries still operate in Japan today. By the late 19th century saké drinking was widespread and the varieties of rice wine available had multiplied to accommodate the widely varying tastes of the Japanese consumer. In fact, during this period the social class of a family was said to be determined by the quality of saké they consumed.[61]

3.1.2. Saké in Modern Times

During the 20th century, both the brewing technology as well as the commercialization of saké advanced steadily. For instance, the use of wooden barrels was discontinued, in favor of easy to clean, enamel-coated steel tanks, allowing breweries to minimize microbial contamination during processing. Modern marketing methods including branding and advertising campaigns were used effectively to popularize saké. The Japanese government supported this growth; they established the first saké-brewing research institute in 1904 and sponsored the first saké competition in 1907. Saké was clearly well poised to enjoy unprecedented growth as the premier beverage in Japan.

The Second World War, however, dampened this growth significantly. Thousands of breweries all over Japan closed abruptly as most of the rice grown during this time was used in the war effort. Interestingly, however, this shortage of rice during the war also resulted in some technical changes in the brewing process. For example, the practice of adding glucose and pure alcohol to the rice mash in order to increase the yield and shorten the brewing time was developed during this period. Brewers had already discovered that adding small amounts of alcohol to saké improved its aroma and texture. By government decree, pure alcohol and glucose were added to the rice mash, increasing the yield by as much as four times. About 95% of the saké in the market today uses this practice that has continued from the war years. There were even a few breweries that produced so-called saké without using any rice at all. Naturally, the quality of saké during this time suffered greatly. It was only after the war that the breweries slowly began to recover, and the quality of saké again gradually improved to its present level. Today, the quality of saké is the best it has ever been and its popularity is increasing worldwide. Currently around 2,000 saké-breweries operate in Japan.

A second important factor that affected saké's lead in the marketplace was the introduction of beer into Japan via its interaction with the West in the early nineteenth century. The new players on the scene; beer, wine, and spirits, also became popular in Japan, and in the 1960s beer consumption surpassed that of saké

---

[60] *Tanimoto, M. & Saito, O., "Zairaisangyo no Saihensei" In Kaiko to Isshin (nihon keizzai shi vol 3) Ed: Yamamoto, Y. and Umemura, M., Tokyou; Iwanami Shoten (1989).*

[61] *Nakanishi, S., Bunmei kaika to minshu seikatsu. In Nihon keizai shi Vol.1; Bakumatsu ishin ki, Ed; Ishi, K., et al., Tokyo University Press (2000).*

for the first time. Saké consumption continued to suffer in the following decades but in contrast the quality of saké still steadily improved. The supply and consumption of saké from 1876 to 1935 are shown in Table 3. The demand for per capita consumption around 1920 to 1925 showed a rapidly increasing rate.

Year	Sake Supply (1000 koku)	Per capita Consumption (liter)
1876	3355	17.0
1880	3460	17.0
1885	3259	15.3
1890	3786	17.1
1895	4642	20.1
1900	4938	20.2
1905	4172	16.1
1910	4794	17.5
1915	4764	16.3
1920	5982	19.2
1925	6331	19.0
1930	5206	14.5
1935	4683	12.2

(From: Inconspicuous Consumption: Sake, Beer and the Birth of Consumerism In Japan, Journal of Asian Studies, 2008).
http://www.e.u-tokyo.ac.jp/cirje/research/workshops/history/history paper2007/Sep 18.pdf

Table 3: Total supply and consumption of saké 1887-1935.

Though the brewing technology of Japanese saké has vastly changed over the centuries, its significance in Japanese life and culture remains virtually unchanged. From its early beginnings in Japan, saké has been a drink associated with respectability, social stature, family values, friendship, and cultural events. Because it is a special beverage to be enjoyed in the company of friends and family, Japanese social etiquette demands saké to be poured out to guests.

3.2. The Raw Materials

Saké is made primarily from rice and water interacting with microbes in the *koji* and saké yeast mix. Thus, the quality and characteristics of each of these crucial elements greatly influence the quality of the saké produced.[62, 63]

3.2.1. Rice

Historically, the land owners who grew rice crops would have rice left over at the end of the season and would ship it to the breweries. But, just as the quality of wine depends on quality of the grapes, making good saké requires a special grade of rice, called *sakamai.* Modern breweries are very particular about the variety of rice

[62] *Saké-The Making and Tradition of Japan's National Beverage. Japan Saké Brewers Association.*

[63] *Akiyama, Y., Nihonshu (Saké), Tokyo, Iwanami Shoten (1994.)*

they use in their brewing process. Each of the several varieties of rice yields produced in a growing season and used for saké-making produces a saké with a distinctively different taste. Japanese rice can be broadly classified into the ordinary rice used as food, and the *sakamai*, used primarily for saké production. *Sakamai* has a larger grain size and is somewhat softer than the ordinary eating rice. While the ordinary rice can also be used, it is the saké made from *sakamai*-rice that has the reputation for high quality. *Sakamai* rice also tends to be relatively more expensive than table rice since it only grows in certain areas of the country and requires more complicated cultivation techniques.

3.2.2. Water

A suitable climate and a clean source of water with the appropriate mineral content are also critical to ensuring the high quality of saké. This is to be expected, as the beverage is more than 80 percent water! Semi-hard water with a low iron and manganese content is generally believed to be best suited for saké-making. Thankfully, Japan has plenty of quality spring water in several regions across the country. As a result, high quality and good-tasting saké can be produced in most regions of Japan.

3.2.3. Koji

Koji, a mix of mold that can convert starch into sugar is one of the crucial ingredients in the saké-brewing process. *Koji*, used for making miso (soy-bean paste) and *shoyu* (soy-sauce) as well, plays a role similar to the mold used in blue cheese production. The know-how in *koji* production is considered to be the "the heart" of the saké-making. In addition to converting the starch to sugar *koji* also contributes to the delicate taste of saké.

3.3. The Saké Manufacturing Process

The brewing process for saké is very different and more complex relative to that for brewed wines. In the latter processes, fermentation initiates when yeast is added to the sugar solution derived from grape or a fruit juice. But the rice starch base used in saké making cannot be fermented with the addition of yeast alone. Saké brewing begins with the introduction of *koji*, which breaks down the rice starch into simple sugars in a process known as "saccharification." Next, the saké yeast is added to initiate the fermentation. This is sometimes referred to as the "multiple parallel fermentation" of polished rice, which is a unique feature of saké-brewing that distinguishes it from other brewed alcoholic wines.

Five crucial elements and factors are involved in the brewing of saké: water, rice, technical skill, yeast, and land/weather. An overview of the saké production process is summarized in Figure 12. This is a generalized description; individual breweries have developed their own proprietary recipes and techniques. However, all of them are based around the following general steps.

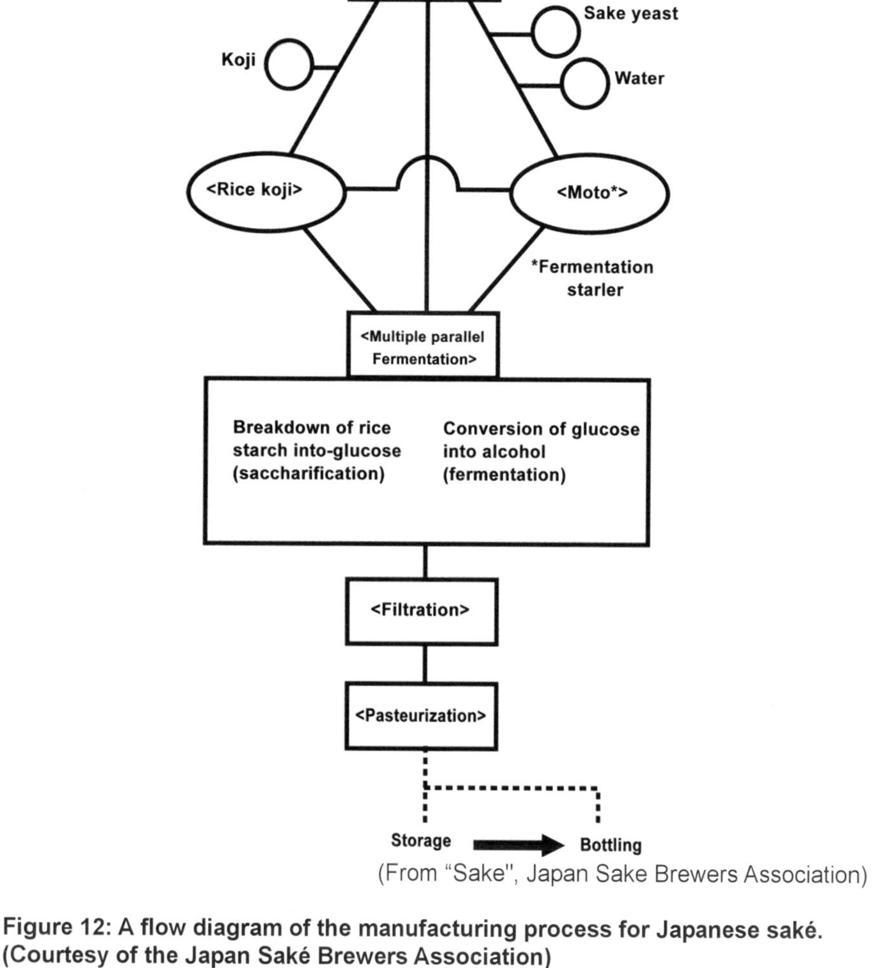

Figure 12: A flow diagram of the manufacturing process for Japanese saké. (Courtesy of the Japan Saké Brewers Association)

The rice is polished, washed and steamed. The steamed rice is allowed to cool down to room temperature and is mixed with the starter of yeast and *koji*. The whole mix is then allowed to ferment under suitable conditions for 18 to 32 days, after which it is pressed, filtered and blended. Even the pressed product can be heavily clouded with residual grain particles and is generally filtered to improve clarity. More details in the saké-making process are now described.

3.3.1. Rice Milling

The rice must be milled, or polished, in order to obtain a good starting base material for saké manufacture. Well-polished rice is generally considered critical to obtaining saké of good quality. This process removes the protein and oils from the exterior of the rice grain, leaving behind the core of complex carbohydrate starch for the most part. However, the milling process must be carried out gently to prevent generating too much heat that will adversely affect the absorption of water by the rice grains. It is also important not to crack the grains as it can interfere with the fermentation process. With early equipment, polishing rice to a predetermined level would not have been that easy. Today there are excellent computer-controlled milling machines that are able to polish off a specified percentage of the outside of the grains. The equipment also minimizes any damage to the rice from frictional heat as well as the incidence of cracked grains.

Washing and Soaking: Milled rice has to be thoroughly washed as this makes a significant difference in the quality of steamed rice. Following that, the rice is soaked to attain a certain water content that is deemed optimum for steaming, for that particular grade of rice. It is the degree to which the rice has been milled hat determines the appropriate water content the rice should have prior to steaming. The more polished the rice is, the faster it absorbs water and the shorter will be the soaking time required. The soaking time needed is quite varied depending on the rice and the degree of milling. It can range from just a few minutes exposure (timed using a stopwatch) to overnight.

Steaming: Steaming in saké manufacture is very different from steaming table rice where the grains are mixed with water and brought to a boil. Instead, the steam is brought in through the bottom of specially-designed vat to work its way through a column of the milled soaked rice. Steaming gives a firmer, slightly harder outer surface and a soft center in the resulting grain of steamed rice. Generally, a batch of steamed rice is divided up into two parts; *koji* mold is sprinkled over a part of the rice and the rest is placed directly in the fermentation vat.

Koji Making (*Seigiku*): This step is at the heart of the entire saké brewing process. Incorporating *koji* usually takes place in a special room with controlled humidity and temperature. *Koji* is used at least four times during the brewing process. It is always made fresh each time it is used and never stored for any length of time. Traditionally, it is hand-made in wood-paneled rooms that are maintained warm and humid. Today, however, the entire process is automated and equipment that closely monitors and controls all aspects of the *koji* making is used for the purpose.

Yeast starter (*Shubo* or *Moto*): A yeast starter, or a seed mash of sorts, is first prepared by mixing the finished *koji* with plain steamed rice, water and a concentration of pure yeast. Yeast grows well in this medium and typically over a two week period the concentration of yeast cells can reach as high as 100 million cells in one teaspoon.

The Mash (Moromi): After being moved to a larger tank, more rice, more *koji* and water are added in three successive stages over a four day period, roughly doubling the size of the batch with each addition. This is the main mash that is fermented over the next 18 to 32 days. The temperature and a host of other factors are monitored and adjusted to create the best conditions needed for this step.

Pressing (Joso): At an appropriate stage in the process, the saké is pressed, and the white remains (called *kasu*) and unfermented solids are recovered as a cake and the clear saké runs off the press. Until the early 1900's saké was pressed by pouring the *moromi* into canvas bags that were then placed in a large wooden box called a *fune*. The lid was then cranked down into the box, squeezing out the saké. Now, in almost all breweries, the process is automated. Saké is pressed in a large accordion-like machine that squeezes the *moromi* between balloon-like inflating panels, at a controlled rate and also allowing the *kasu* to be recovered easily for disposal.

*3.3.2. Filtration (*Roka*) and Pasteurization*

After sitting for a few days to let the fine solids settle out, saké is usually charcoal filtered to adjust its flavor and color. This is done to different degrees at different breweries depending on the subtle characteristics of the saké desired.

Saké is pasteurized once by heating the brew rapidly and passing it through a pipe immersed in hot water. This kills off any bacteria and deactivates enzymes that may further act on the saké, that may lead to adverse flavor or color during storage. Saké that is not pasteurized called *namazake* is also available; it maintains a certain unique freshness in its flavor but must be kept refrigerated.

Aging: Finally, most saké is left to age for a short period of about six months before distribution, rounding out the flavor. It is generally diluted with pure water to adjust the alcohol level from near 20% down to 16% or so, and thereby also blended to ensure consistency. It may be pasteurized a second time at this stage. It is somewhat unfair to the saké-brewing craft and industry to reduce saké brewing down to the short explanation above, but a more detailed technical discussion of the process is beyond the scope of this book.

3.4. Different Types of Saké

As shown in Table 4, many different types saké are commercially available in Japan. However, in general, there are five basic types of saké. Each of these is brewed slightly differently using rice that is milled to different levels, and therefore each has its own distinct characteristics.

Type of Sake	Material	Rice-polishing	Rate of Malted rice	Character
Jumai-Daiginjyo-shu	Rice, Malted rice	Under 50%	Over 15%	Distinctive aroma, Excellent color with luster
Daiginjyo-shu	Rice, Malted rice Alcohol	Under 50%	Over 15%	Distinctive aroma, Excellent color with luster
Junmai-Ginjyo-shu	Rice, Malted rice	Under 60%	Over 15%	Distinctive aroma, Excellent color with luster
Ginjyo-shu	Rice, Malted rice	Under 60%	Over 15%	Distinctive aroma, Good color with luster
Junmai-shu	Rice, Malted rice		Over 15%	Fine aroma, Good color with luster
Tokubetsu Junmai-shu	Rice, Malted rice	Under 60% or Specially	Over 15%	
Honjyozo-shu	Rice, Malted rice Alcohol	Under 70%	Over 70%	Fine aroma, Good color with luster
Tokubetsu Honjyozo-shu	Rice, Malted rice Alcohol	Under 60% or Specially processed	Over15%	Excellently fine aroma, Excellent color with luster

Alcohol referred to here is the one obtained from distillation of fermented starches and sugars.
(From "What's Nada no Sake?". Nada no sake for Health and Beauty, Nadagogo Sake Brewers' Association, P.10.)

Table 4: The characteristics of the different classes of Japanese saké.

Junmai-shu: This type is made from saké rice but without adding any brewing alcohol.

Junmai-shu means 'pure saké', with no adjuncts or alcohol added. *Junmai-shu* often has a fuller, richer body and a higher than average level of acidity.

Honjyozo-shu: This type is made from milled or polished saké rice, with at least 30% of the exterior of each rice grain milled away. A small amount of distilled pure alcohol is usually added during brewing. *Honjyozo-shu* is considered somewhat lighter than other types of saké due to the small amount of distilled pure alcohol added at the end of the fermentation. *Honjyozo-shu* makes a good candidate for warm saké.

Ginjyo-shu: This type is made from milled or polished rice where at least 40% of the exterior of the rice grains is polished away, and either with or without distilled pure alcohol being added during processing. If the bottle is labeled *Ginjyo*, it signifies that distilled alcohol was added and, if labeled *Junmai Ginjyo*, that no alcohol was added. *Ginjyo-shu* is much more delicate, light and complex in flavor compared to *Honjyozo-shu* or *Junmai-shu*.

Daiginjyo-shu: This is a grade made from heavily milled or polished rice, with at least 50% of the exterior of the rice grains polished away. Again, a small amount of distilled pure alcohol may or may not be used in the processing. *Daiginjyo-shu* represents the highest and finest quality of saké. If bottle is labeled *Daiginjyo*, it signifies that brewing alcohol was added and if labeled *Junmai Daiginjyo*, that no alcohol was added during manufacture.

Namazake: *Namazake* is unpasteurized saké. It should be stored cold, or the flavor and clarity could rapidly deteriorate. *Namazake* has a fresh, lively touch in its flavor. Any of the types of saké mentioned above can be processed without pasteurization and can then be classified as *namazake*.

Jo-con-shu: This is concentrated saké derived from *Junmai-shu* saké. *Jo-con-shu* is frozen at a low temperature (-30C) to raise its alcohol content (38.5%) and matured for a minimum of six months after fermentation to develop and deep flavor.[64] The amino acids level also doubles during this process increasing the acidity to flavor about twice that of the standard saké, making it more "food-friendly." Even when diluted, it maintains its original taste.

3.5. Saké Labels

Today, there are as many as 2,000 registered saké breweries in Japan marketing under 1,500 brands. Moreover, since most breweries make several grades or types of saké, there are likely to be as many as 10,000 different varieties of saké made in Japan. Compared to wine or beer labels, saké labels contain a great deal of information, such as the type and taste of saké (dry, sweet, etc.), the brewmaster's name, the date the batch was produced, the kinds of rice used, etc. For those interested in more details, the degree to which the rice was polished, saké meter values (i.e. the specific gravity), and the acidity can also be found on the label. Knowing more about the saké adds to the satisfaction in consuming it.

3.6. The Taste of Saké

There are many ways to assess the flavor profile of saké. Figure 13 summarizes the relationship between the taste and fragrance of saké. Like with any premium beverage, saké has a wide range of flavors and fragrances, each person is said to taste and smell something a little bit different in any given type of saké. As with wine, one of the easiest ways to classify saké is based on the sweetness and dryness, which is mainly determined by the balance between the sugar and acid levels in the finished product. In the so-called "heavy/dry" grades of saké both the sugar and acid contents are high. High levels of acids can knock out the sweetness, creating a dry saké. If the available acid is not sufficient to downplay the sugars, the saké tastes sweet. But when the overall sugar content is too low, flavor suffers, and the saké tastes rather watery and dilute. Good-quality saké with a clean flavor results from a well-balanced mix of sugar and acids.

---

[64] *This saké can be enjoyed as an excellent aperitif or after a meal, or of course to accompany a fine. http//www.jo~con.jp*

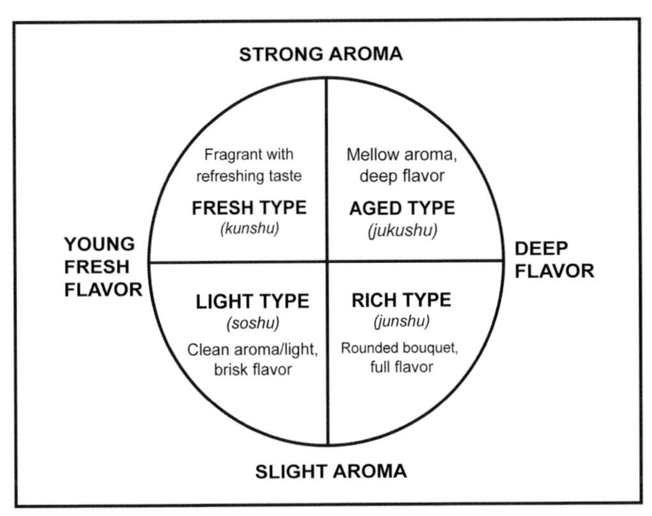

(From Harper, P., "The Insider's Guide to Sake., Kodansha International, p58, 1998) According to the position established along these axes, a Sake is considered to be of "mature type," "fragrant type," "light and smooth type," or "full-bodied type.

Figure 13: The basic relationship between the fragrance and the taste of saké.

3.7. Saké as an Accompaniment to Food

Saké can be served cold or warm as well as hot. Typically, it is consumed warm in winter and cold in the summer. Saké is an alcoholic beverage to be enjoyed with many different kinds of food. As shown in Glance 2, saké tastes particularly good with Japanese food. Saké is not only able to soften the strong smell of raw seafood (such as that of raw fish in Japanese dishes such as sushi or sashimi), but saké also brings out the full flavor of such dishes. Saké is therefore also widely used for preparing and seasoning Japanese (and some Western) dishes. Today, saké is no longer considered compatible just with Japanese food, but is also highly regarded as a beverage to accompany almost any of the world's cuisines.

(From "Sake", Japan Sake Brewers Association)

Saké brewing begins with the introduction of *Koji*, which break down rice starch binto glucose in a process known as saccharinification. Next, saké yeast is added and fermentation begins. This process, in which saccharinification and fermentation take place in the same vat at the same time, is called "multiple parallel fermentation."

Glance 2: A bird's-eye view of the saké production process.

In general, sweeter grades of saké are more compatible with sweet dishes and the dry (*karakuchi)* grades go particularly well with soy sauce-based food. For instance, for dishes that contain sweeteners or are potato -based, a sweet grade of saké is often a good selection. Salty dishes on the other hand require a dry grade of saké. With heavy and rich dishes a full-bodied, rich grade of saké is recommended. This combination brings alive the flavor in both the saké and the food. Conversely, a lightly seasoned dish should generally be accompanied by lighter saké.

Matching different varieties or grades of saké with types of food or with particular dishes is ultimately a matter of personal experience and preference. Following are some general guidelines followed by the author. Discovering the favorite combinations that best suit your own palate is important as well as entertaining.

Sushi and Sashimi: A soy sauce-based food. Dry saké recommended.

Yakitori: A salty dish. Dry or rich grades of saké match this dish well. If dipping yakitori in sauce (tare), a moderate to sweet saké is particularly compatible, Salted yakitori (no sauce) always goes well with the dry saké.

Tempura: A soy sauce-based food that goes particularly well with light and dry saké. With tempura, it is most important to consider how oily the dish is when matching it with a saké. However, because a dipping sauce is often used, sweetness also must be taken into account. To neutralize the oiliness, a dry, light, saké is often the best. If the tempura is dipped in sauce, which has a hint of sweetness, sweet saké would be more appropriate. If eating tempura salted, a light grade of saké that balances the saltiness of the dish provides an excellent match.

Shabu shabu: A food dipped in ponzu (rice vinegar base) or sweet sesame sauces. The recommendation here is to start with a rich saké and then switch to a lighter variety. In either case, sweet saké will be an excellent choice to accompany the dish. A sweet saké will not only match the sweet seasoning such as a sesame sauce but also the strongly acidic seasonings, such as *ponzu*.

Sukiyaki: Prepared by cooking slices of beef, onions and other vegetables in a shallow pan, flavored with sweetened saké, soy-sauce and sugar. Here a sweet saké is recommended.

Chinese food: Here too it is best to start with a light saké and switch to a richer variety later in the meal. Although Chinese food is often claimed to be oily, it uses a wide variety of cooking methods and ingredients. A dry light saké may not always prove to be the best match. With a light Chinese appetizer, as with sashimi, a light saké is best. If the dish is covered in a sweet, thick sauce, it is best to start with light saké, then switch to a richer-sweet variety later in the meal.

Chapter 4: Getting Along with Saké

The Japanese believe that regular consumption of fresh locally grown seasonal produce along with their saké to be an excellent strategy to ensure good health. In the summer months Japanese diners enjoy fresh cucumber with cold saké to beat the summer heat. During the autumn, Japanese feast on nutritious sanma (mackerel pike) drunken with delectably rich varieties of saké, as the people prepare to face the cold winter months to come. In the winter, nabe (one-pot cooking) served with hot saké warms the body and soul. A natural harmony exists between the seasonal varieties of food enjoyed by the Japanese along with good health and longevity. It is certainly not an exaggeration to attribute the well-known longevity of the Japanese to this combination of nutritious and seasonal traditional Japanese food and the saké consumed with it.

Throughout its long history, the consumption of saké has been associated with beautiful skin tone, and beauty itself. Even today, many believe that those who work regularly in the saké breweries have smooth, beautiful hands, and that beautiful women with clear skins are commonly found in the areas famous for saké breweries. Saké in Japan is therefore regarded as being synonymous with health and beauty, as well as pleasure.

4.1. Celebrating Saké

Saké is often served where people gather in any public or social event in Japan. In these gatherings it is common to see the older men in the community wander around the crowd with large bottles of saké and paper cups, pouring the beverage out generously. Sometimes, great casks of saké are opened, their wooden tops ceremoniously smashed with wooden mallets and the saké distributed freely to those gathered. It is important to appreciate, however, that the objective of drinking saké at these occasions is never to get intoxicated but rather to intermingle socially.

Saké has become an indispensable part of everyday life in Japan. Interestingly, it has also become a key element in Japan's most prominent religion, Shinto. In keeping with the Shinto tradition most Japanese believe in deities or god/sprits called *Kami-sama*. In the ancient Shinto beliefs *Kami-sama* are said to exist throughout the universe, providing guidance or control over everything and everyone. Each of the many Shinto shrines in Japan is associated with its own special *Kami-sama*. Devotees generally offer gifts and worship the *Kami-sama* at these shrines. This often involves purification rituals by a priest, after which those gathered would share the saké, called *Omiki*, which is ceremoniously served to the deities. Serving saké at these rituals is believed to forge a special connection between the *Kami-sama* and the participants.

Similarly, at most Japanese wedding ceremonies, the time-honored 3-3-9 ritual is performed, where the bride and the groom drink *Omiki* as a part of taking their marital vows. Each drinks three times from each of three bowls, consuming a total of 9 sips of the saké. At the end of the ceremony, relatives and well-wishers also share the *Omiki*, symbolically recognizing and honoring the newly formed family connections.

4.2. Saké as an Accompaniment to Food

As mentioned, saké is best enjoyed with Japanese and Chinese cuisine, as shown in Glance 3. However, saké is also being served in upscale non-Asian restaurants all over the world.

(From "Sake", Japan Sake Brewers Association)

Why not give yourself a treat and explore the exotic, profound world of Sake? Kanpai!!! (Cheers!)

Glance 3: Saké as an accompaniment for a meal.

Saké is an ideal beverage to accompany almost any of the world's cuisines, regardless of the ingredients or the style of preparation. This explains why it is often served at leading French and Italian restaurants in Japan. Saké not only enhances the flavor but also softens the strong smell of meats or the seafood, bringing out the full essence of these dishes. It therefore goes particularly well with sashimi as well as with fish and egg dishes (for instance, salmon roe and cod roe). Today, saké is hardly a drink to be enjoyed just with sushi or sashimi.

Saké brewed in various parts of Japan has always been a distinctive part of the Japanese cuisine. It is traditionally enjoyed with the popular local woodland delicacies as well as those freshly caught from the sea and rivers. As might be expected, certain varieties of saké go better with particular Japanese dishes. The basic tenet to remember when matching saké and food is that "light saké goes well with light food, and heavy varieties of saké go with the richer food." For instance, lighter grades of saké should be enjoyed with sashimi of whitefish or shellfish, while the richer grades are best relished with well-seasoned dishes such as broiled fish, yakitori and roast beef. If the saké is a fragrant variety, it will go very well with seafood cooked with seasonings such as orange peel and herbs.

In general, sweeter saké is a great accompaniment for sweet dishes and the dry (*karakuti*) saké goes better with soy sauce-based food preparations. Dishes that are sweet or use starches such as potatoes are best served with a sweet light saké. The full-bodied, richer grades of saké are only served with the richest dishes. These combinations work well because they work synergistically, bringing out the flavor of both the saké and the food. Depending on personal experience and choices, other guidelines on how to match saké with food might be derived. But the most important and time-honored of these is that one should discover one's own favorite food choices and combinations for enjoying saké.

Some general guidelines for matching saké with Japanese food were published[65] by Sushi and Saké magazines. The applications are summarized in Table 5. These are by no means strict rules to adhere to but an interesting starting point. The reader is encouraged to experiment and find combinations that best suit him and his company.

	Food Type	Sake Type
1	Sweet food	Sweet and dry sake
2	Rich food	Rich full-bodied sake (Yakitori)
3	Fishy or gamey foods	Rich full-bodied sake
4	Acidic food	Sweet sake
5	Plain food	Ginjyo sake
6	Greasy food	Refined or aged sake
7	Salty food	Dry sake(Sushi, sashimi or tempura)

https//chartreuse.site-secure.net/sushiandtofu/sushi_and_tofu/food_sakeWithFood_0601.htm

Table 5: Some recommended saké-food combinations.

In discussing how to match saké with different types of food, we have introduced the basic concepts of saké characteristics: sweetness, dryness, richness, and aroma, as well as the food characteristics of sweetness, saltiness and oiliness. In doing so we have proposed several different combinations or ways of serving it, to enjoy saké, but it is important to appreciate that personal preferences override all such guidelines. Despite the guidelines what works best for one's palate is ultimately the best combination of saké and a meal.

Cooking with saké (*Ryori-shu*): Just as with wine some grades of saké are used exclusively for cooking. A recently developed strain of rice just for use in manufacturing cooking saké (*ryori-shu*) has been developed and in recent years has drawn a lot of attention in Japan. The *ryori-shu* saké made by the Oki brewery (Fukushima, Japan) *junmai-shu* is known for its a very high amino acids content and concentration of *umami* (deliciousness). For instance, the *Konnichiwa ryori-shu* has four times the amino acids content of normal brands of saké. This highly concentrated, sweet-flavored, *ryori-shu* can easily suppress the fishy odor of seafood and the heavy

---

[65] *https://charteuse.sitesecure.net/sushiandtofu/sushi_and_tofu_SakéWithFood_0601.htm*

smell of cooked meat, bringing out the flavor of each ingredient and possibly helping preserve the food as well.

4.3. Enjoying Saké, Hot or Cold

As mentioned, saké is an alcoholic beverage that can be served cold, warm or hot, depending on personal preference. Also preference of course runs as well to the quality and the type of the saké, and the season in which it is enjoyed. As might be expected, hot saké is typically favored in the winter season and cold saké in the summer months (Glance 4). It is a common misconception that all saké should necessarily be served warm; there are a few varieties that are best served at the cooler temperatures.

(From "Sake", Japan Sake Brewers Association)

Glance 4: Elegant ways of serving saké. Should saké be enjoyed hot or cold?

Shipping hot saké from a favorite cup in hand would be a real pleasure only matured people could appreciate. Served hot, Sake becomes more aromatic and its taste grows thicker saké is also served at room temperature (*Hiya*) or chilled (*Reishu*). Aromatic types of saké are said no better suited for drinking at low temperatures.

Warm or hot saké, referred to in Japan as "*kanzake,*" has been enjoyed in Japan for hundreds of years. The higher temperature of the drink is believed to increase the physiological impact of the alcohol in saké, which perhaps explains why most who enjoy warm saké believe that it "packs a punch." But in reality, most varieties of saké have only about 16 percent alcohol, a level similar to that in wines. The higher temperature at which it is served, the faster the rate of absorption of the alcohol into the body will be.

The flavor of the saké as well as its dryness increases with the temperature at which it is served. Because it increases the dryness of the beverage, warm or hot saké is the perfect companion for plain foods such as *sashimi* (raw fish) or *sushi*. The dryness also helps to mask the oiliness of hot pot dishes made with fat s or oils.

The best way to prepare warm or hot saké is to place the *tokkuri* (jar), the ceramic flask used to serve the saké, in a bowl of hot water heated to almost the boiling point. The duration of heating varies depending on the desired serving temperature of the saké. Generally, warm saké should be served at about 40C (104 degree F) and a good visual cue to judge this is to observe the *tokkuri* during the heating process. If the bubbles accumulate on the sides of the *tokkuri*, but do not rise to the surface, the saké is warm (*nurukan*). If the bubbles do rise to the surface, the saké is hot (*joukan*). One can in theory also use a microwave oven to heat saké, but the risk of boiling it accidentally makes it less desirable. Boiling would, of course, ruin the delicate flavor of saké.

Warm or hot saké is the perfect companion for sashimi or sushi as well as Japanese *nabe* (one-pot cooking). Chilled or cold saké that has been cooled in the refrigerator is referred to as *reishu* or *hiyazake*. Cold saké is generally served in the hot summer season and is a good accompaniment for sweet and sour dishes. However, the delicate flavor of saké can sometimes be altered if served at an inappropriate temperature. How does one decide to serve saké warm, hot or cold? An important guideline here is that the serving temperature depends on the quality of the saké, as is evident from Table 6. Any saké that has had distilled alcohol added to it is best served warm or hot, because it enhances food flavors. However, the better grades of saké are usually better served cold.

Type	Temperature°F		
Very Hot	133	Heated	Full-bodied Kimoto & Yamaha sake
Slightly Hot	122	Heated	Full-bodied Kimoto & Yamaha sake
Warm	113	Heated	Full-bodied Kimoto & Yamaha sake
Body temperature	95	Normal	Acidic, medium-bodied aroma sake
Colder	59-41	Chilled	Light-bodied, highly fragrant sake Acidic, medium-bodied sake

(From Matsumoto, Y. "Sushi and Sake, March, 2008 Issue")

Table 6: Serving Temperature for Saké.

In addition to the traditional methods of serving saké, either warm or cold, creating saké-based cocktails have also recently increased in popularity. As with different food and saké combinations, one should also experiment with different grades of saké, and the temperatures at which it is served, as well as with different mixed drinks in order to discover his or her personal preference. Some cocktails using saké are suggested as a starting point for the reader in Glance 5.

Samurai Rock

Pour 60 c.c. of saké and 10 c.c. of lime syrup on the cracked ice in the drinking glass and stir gently. Fresh lime juice instead of (or in addition to) lime syrup will make the drink more refreshing.

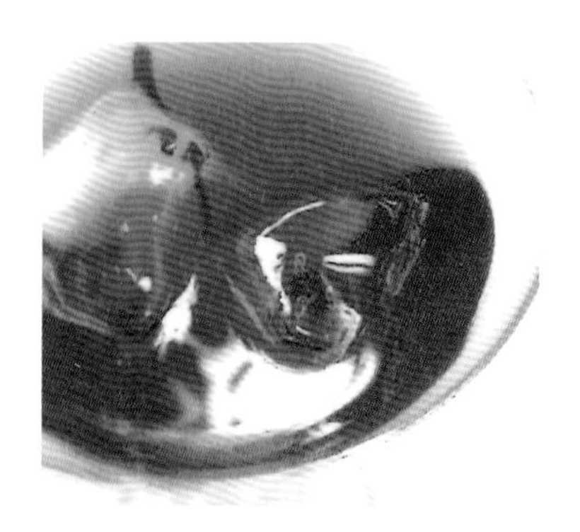

Parisian
Mix up 45 c.c. of saké, 30 c.c. of dry gin and 15 c.c. of cassis liqueur in the mixing glass. Pour the mixture into the drinking glass and put a cherry on it.

Old Fashion
Pour 60 c.c. of saké and 10 c.c. of carbonated water on a lump sugar and cracked ice in the drinking glass. A slice of lemon, a slice of orange and/or a cherry can be added.

Sake Ginger
Pour 10 c.c. of lemon juice onto 60 c.c. of saké on the rocks, and add some ginger ale. Put a slice of lemon and mint leaves as decoration.

Ringo Star
Pour 60 c.c. of chilled saké, apple juice about two or three times the amount of saké and a little bit of carbonated water on the cracked ice in the drinking glass. Stir lightly and serve.

Sunset
Pour 60 c.c. of saké and 180 c.c. of tomato juice on the cracked ice in the drinking glass and stir. Decorate with a slice of lemon and a small rib of celery.

(From "Nada no Sake for Health and Beauty")

Sake can be a good base for cocktails with mild taste and rich flavor.

Glance 5: Healthy cocktails based on Japanese saké.

Sipping chilled water at intervals while drinking saké is recommended primarily because it lowers the blood alcohol concentration and helps to avoid quick intoxication. The water also rinses the mouth, allowing one to better savor the following mouthful of saké, as well as the next morsel of food. The chilled water is called *yawaragi-mizu* (softening water), implying the 'softening" of the intoxicating effects of alcohol.

4.4. Saké Etiquette

When serving saké as an aperitif, it is customary to use a traditional serving set consisting of a small porcelain pitcher and several small cups usually shaped like little bowls. Serving sets, however, come in a variety of shapes and are generally made of ceramic or wood. Serving saké is almost a ritual in Japan. One of the most important rules of traditional saké etiquette is that it is improper to pour saké for yourself. Instead, each person at the table serves one or more others and vice versa. The server holds the pitcher with both hands when pouring out saké, while the person being served holds their cup with one hand and supports the bottom of the cup with the other hand.

In many social settings, this ritual is only observed for the first round of drinks served, but it still adds a special level of intimacy to gatherings of family or friends. Saké has been traditionally served warm in ceramic serving sets. Saké chilled or at room temperature is traditionally served in a wooden set. Saké sets are often elaborate, artistically designed and created with meticulous care. In some parts of the world they have become a collector items.

Whether you prefer to drink saké by itself or in one of the many new mixed drinks, the best place to enjoy saké in Japan is probably izakaya. The izakaya. is essentially a traditional bar that provides various Japanese-style snacks, which go very well with any kind of saké. In general, the prices of the drinks in an *izakaya* are much lower than in formal restaurants, and the atmosphere is far more casual. Serving sets used in an *izakaya* come in a variety of shapes and materials, but are generally of ceramic, called *o-choko*. As already described, to warm the saké, immerse the *tokkuri*, the ceramic flask used to serve the beverage, in boiling water served in a pan.

Drinking in groups starts with the traditional *kampai* (cheers!). It is impolite to place a freshly poured out cup on the table without first drinking from it. On receiving a cup of saké at least a single sip must be enjoyed before putting it down. Another important custom in drinking saké is to never drink the entire cupful at once; always leave about half the amount of saké in the cup. It is polite however to empty your cup just before receiving a refill offer of another cup of saké from another. In a group it is also polite to periodically check to make sure that one's companions' cups are not empty. If someone moves to refill your cup and you do not wish to drink any more, you can always politely decline the offer.

4.5. A Glossary of Seasonal Words for Saké Drinking

Saké has become an essential and indispensable part of Japanese festivals. Some of the events and festivals at which serving saké is traditional are listed below.

Spring

Hina matsuri (March 3): The Festival of Dolls. Also called Girl's Day Festival, this is the day to wish future happiness to females. Sets of dolls dressed in traditional costumes worn in the royal court in ancient times, decorated with peach blossoms, are displayed. A sweet drink called *sirozake* brewed from rice gruel mixed with fermented rice is traditionally served on this day.

Tango no sekku (May 5): This is the corresponding Boys' Festival where young men receive wishes that each of them in their family will grow up to be healthy and strong. Warrior figures are set up in the house during this festival, iris leaves are placed under the eaves to fend off evil, and huge fish-like streamers are fastened to poles. Special rice cakes wrapped in oak leaves and *shobu-saké* (oak leaves saké) are traditionally served on this day.

Summer

Tanabata (July 7): The Star Festival is held on the evening of the 7th of July each year. The festival traces its origins to a legend that the Cowherd Star (Altair) and Weaver Star (Vega) were lovers separated by the Milky Way, and are allowed to meet just once a year, on the seventh day of the seventh month. People write their wishes down on narrow strips of colored paper and hang them, along with other paper ornaments, on bamboo branches placed in the backyards or at the entrances to their homes. They pray fervently that their wishes will come true. The *Tanabata* festival is thought to have originated in China. It was transmitted to Japan during the feudal period and combined with traditional local customs to become an official event at the Imperial court. Commoners soon began observing this festival, with different localities developing their own distinctive ways of celebrating.

Obon (around mid August): *Obon* is the festival of souls, an annual Buddhist event for commemorating one's ancestors. It is believed that each year during *Obon*, ancestors' spirits return to this world in order to visit their relatives. Traditionally, lanterns are hung in front of homes to guide these spirits, *Obon* dances (*bon odori*) are performed, graves are visited and food offerings are made at altars in homes and in temples. At the end of *Obon*, the lanterns are floated down rivers, lakes and the sea in order to guide the spirits back into their own world. *Obon* is celebrated in mid August in many regions of Japan. The *Obon* week in mid August is one of Japan's three major holiday seasons, accompanied by intensive domestic and international travel activities. Travel costs and accommodation in Japan peaks around this time.

Autumn

Tsukimi (nights of the full moon on August 15 and September 13 of the lunar calendar): the days for "moon gazing." Decorations of Japanese pampas grass are commonly used during this period, and moon-offerings of *tsukimi-saké* and *dan*go (a kind of dumpling are prepared for the enjoyment of those gazing at the moon in the autumn evenings.

Respect-for-the-Aged Day (the third Monday of September): This is a special day set aside to pay respect and affection for the elderly who have devoted most of their life for the benefit of the society for so many years, and for celebrating their long life. In cities, towns and villages, the elderly are invited to be entertained and are given gifts to mark the occasion.

Winter

Ganjitsu (January 1): On the first day of the year the birth of the New Year is celebrated. Japanese observe a three-day holiday at the beginning of the New Year, the period being called *sanga nichi*, or *shougatsu*. They visit shrines, friends and relatives, drink *toso* (special saké drunk in celebration of the New Year), or *shougatsu-saké,* and eat special new year dishes, called *osechi*.

4.6. Side Dishes to Enjoy with Saké

Japan is rich in both marine and farm products. This is primarily responsible for the unique, delicious and elegant Japanese cuisine perfected over generations to a point of high excellence. The majority of these dishes are contrived to accentuate the delicate flavor of fresh fish and shellfish, and almost all of the dishes are designed to go well with rice and saké. The season of the year is a prime factor not only in selecting the food item but also choice in preparing them for the table.

Japanese people usually eat three meals a day. It is at the dinner table that we eat the most substantial meal of the day. Ordinarily an adult man drinks a bottle of beer before dinner, or one or two *go* of saké (one *go* is about 180 ml). In cooking and serving the food, housewives pay special attention not only to the nutritional balance of the meal but also the blend of color and geometric arrangement of the food on plates. A minimum of three dishes are served at dinner (at special occasions it can be more than five), together with a bowl of clear soup and rice. Some of the typical Japanese dishes are: sashimi (slice of raw fish), *yaki-zakana* (broiled fish), *nimono* (fish or vegetables cooked in soy-sauce), tempura (deep fried foods), *oshitashi* (boiled greens with soy-sauce), and *tsukemono* (pickles and salted vegetables).

One *go* of saké has about the same calorific values as a bowl of steamed rice. The risk of obesity depends on the total caloric values we take from saké and its side dishes. Clearly over-indulgence in either saké or the food needs to be avoided.

One way to ensure this is to select side dishes that are low in calorific value and high in protein level. Such foods include tofu (bean curd), sashimi, vegetables and seaweeds. Selecting a mix of side dishes that are cooked in different ways from deep-fried, grilled and stewed to marinated is recommended.

Saké has always been an essential part of the life of Japanese and as an accompaniment to food it can bestow valuable health benefits. The daily diet in Japan has traditionally been considered as consisting of a main, or staple, item of food supplemented by subsidiary items. The best healthy selections as accompaniments to saké are listed below.

During the Whole Year

1) Freshly made *tofu*, as *hiyayakko* or *yudofu*
2) Properly made homemade *nukazuke*
3) Freshly made, piping hot crispy *tempura*
4) *Mentaiko* or *tarako*
5) Assorted fresh-as possible *sashimi*
6) *Ika no shiokara*
7) Fresh seaweed *sunomono* (can also have some *tako* in it)
8) *Ikura* or *sujiko*
9) Goma *dofu*
10) *Chawan mushi* or *tamago dofi,* either piping hot or ice cold
11) *Gindara no kasuzuke*
12) *Surume*
13) *Nikujaga*
14) Spinach *gomaae*
15) *Yakitori*
16) *Kamaboko*
17) *Buta no kakuni*
18) Stewed *kiriboshi daikon*
19) *Konnyaku no dengaku*
20) *Sukiyaki*

Spring

1) *Fuki no tou*
2) Goya *champuruu*

Summer

1) *Yakinasu* with grated ginger
2) *Edamame*
3) *Yakinasu* with grated ginger

Autumn

1) Very fresh *sanma* (saury), sizzling hot from the grill, eaten with a drizzle of soy sauce and a mound of grated *daikon* radish
2) A whole grilled wild Japanese *matutake*
3) *Yamakake*, grated *yamaimo* with *maguro* (red tuna) cubes (or just *tororo* with a raw egg)
4) *Hakusaizuke*
5) *Kiritanpo*

Winter

1) *Kakifurai*
2) *Ankou nabe*
3) *Kazunoko*
4) *Tazukuri*

Substitute for Staple Foods

1) Freshly made *sobagaki* with *sobayu*
2) *Unadon*
3) Freshly made *mochi*, with *kinako* and sugar, grated *daikon* and soy sauce or *natto*
4) *Inarizushi*
5) *Tamago kake gohan*
6) *Sauce Yakisoba*
7) *Oyako donburi*

Chapter 5: Social Concerns Regarding the Negative Impacts of Alcohol

5.1. Juvenile Drinking (Zero Tolerance Policy)

Addictive excessive consumption of alcohol is a serious social concern in Japan. Among adults, the problem is particularly serious with middle-aged Japanese males. Alcohol consumption by this group is generally higher in Japan compared to that of ethnic Japanese living in the US.[66] Cultural norms in Japan are tolerant of male drinking but very much against women or minors drinking alcohol. It is not uncommon to see drunken men late at night in downtown areas of major Japanese cities; such intoxication generally does not lead to violence or crime. Habitual overconsumption, however, is serious. A blood alcohol level over 0.4% is lethal and can result from consuming about 2 liters of saké. There is some recent evidence that alcohol consumption by Japanese women is also on the increase.[67]

The Japanese law sets 20 years as the minimum drinking age (Law Prohibiting Minors from Drinking). Particularly serious is the increase in underage drinking that is not only illegal but is also socially unacceptable in Japan. Drinking, especially in youth, often leads to undesirable behavior, such as violence or illegal drug use, excessive cigarette smoking, and casual sexual intercourse. Consumption of alcohol in juvenile years is statistically associated with an increased likelihood of developing alcoholism later in life.

A 1992 a survey of 14,000 high school students in Japan revealed the surprising extent of this problem; 80% of high school students admitted to regularly consuming alcohol, with 25% of boys and 11% of girls even claiming to experience blackouts from excessive drinking more than once a week. More recent surveys, however present encouraging findings. A study by Suzuki et al.[68] comparing the drinking habits of 120,000 junior and senior high school students in 1996, 2000 and 2004 found a decreasing trend in alcohol consumption. Japanese society over the past decade has emphasized the prohibition on adolescent drinking, by revising the Law Prohibiting Minors Drinking and increasing the penalties for driving while intoxicated. This may explain this downward trend.

5.2. Alcohol-Related Traffic Accidents

As in other parts of the world, the incidence of alcohol-related traffic accident has been a long-standing problem in Japan as well. Alcohol–related traffic accidents statistically involve more drivers aged 16 to 20, compared to those aged 21 or older.

---

[66] Higuchi, *S., et al., Between age and drinking patterns and drinking problems among Japanese, Japanese-Americans, and Caucasians. Alcoholism: Clinical and Experimental Research, 18 (2), 305, 2006.*

[67] *Higuchi, S., et al., Young People's Drinking Behavior in Japan, (2008). www.icap.org/portals/0/download/Kobe/Higuchi_WASP.pdf*

[68] *Suzuki,K., et al., Decreases in Japanese adolescent drinking in 1996, 2000 and 2004 national surveys of Japanese junior and senior high school students.* Nihon Arukoru Yakubutsu Igakkai Zasshi. Jun; 42 (3): 138, 2007.

The irresponsible combination of alcohol with driving is considered to be one of the most devastating of present day social problems. The increased chance of an accident when driving while impaired is well known and widely researched. Studies have shown that alcohol use is the most important risk factor for fatality in traffic accidents. About 10,000 Japanese die in traffic accidents every year, and about a ninth of these deaths are due to alcohol consumption. For instance, nearly 14,000 drunken driving accidents were reported in 2006, involving 707 fatalities. This is despite the fact that Japan has zero tolerance policy on drunk driving. According to the Road Traffic Act a driver can be convicted if their blood alcohol level is above 0.5 mg/ml or above 0.25 mg/l in exhaled air, and if a driver is judged to be in a drunken state by a sobriety test. Recent changes in the law make it illegal even to be a passenger in a car operated by an alcohol-impaired driver.

5.3. Alcohol Dependence and Alcoholism

The serious health effects that can result from habitual undue consumption of saké or any other alcohol are well known. These include alcoholic psychosis, alcohol dependence syndrome, alcohol abuse, alcoholic polyneuropathy, alcoholic cardiomyopathy, alcoholic gastritis, alcoholic liver cirrhosis, ethanol toxicity and methanol toxicity. Other ailments where alcohol may play a crucial causal role include oesophageal varices, unspecified cirrhosis, chronic pancreatitis, road injuries, fall injuries, fire injuries, drowning, suicide and homicide. Alcohol abuse can also have secondary harmful effects on non-users as well; victims of alcohol-related traffic accident or violence, or families of drinkers who may suffer economic hardship as a result, belong to this category.

Alcohol dependence is not only a destructive and devastating experience for the individual but also a serious problem for their family, associates and friends.

Alcoholism is said to have set in when the level of consumption begins to interfere with one's physical health, mental health, and social, family, or occupational responsibilities. Alcoholism is essentially a form of drug addiction. A central descriptive characteristic of the alcohol dependence syndrome is "clear addiction to alcohol." There are physical and psychological components of this addiction. Alcohol affects the central nervous system as a depressant, resulting in a decrease of activity, memory loss, anxiety, tension, and inhibitions. Even a few drinks can result in behavioral changes, a slowing down of motor performance, and a decrease in the ability to think clearly wherein concentration and judgment become impaired.

Alcohol can also result in serious physiological changes. These include the irritation of the gastrointestinal tract that can cause nausea and vomiting, and possible bleeding. Absorption of some vitamins might be compromised and possibly lead to nutritional deficiencies due to the long-term users of alcohol. A liver disease, called alcoholic hepatitis, may develop and progress on to cirrhosis. The heart muscle may be affected. Sexual dysfunction may also occur, causing problems with erections in men and cessation of menstruation in women.

The social consequences of problem drinking or alcohol dependence can be as serious as the medical problems already discussed. Those addicted to alcohol generally have a higher incidence of unemployment, domestic violence, and problems with the law. The development of dependence on alcohol may occur slowly, through many years, following a relatively consistent pattern. At first, with habitual overconsumption a tolerance of alcohol may develop. This triggers consumption of even larger quantities of alcohol in order to reach satiation. The brain soon physically adapts to the presence of alcohol and will not function adequately in its absence.

There is no known medical cause of alcoholism. However, several sociological factors appear to play a role in its development. A person who has an alcoholic parent is generally more likely to become an alcoholic than a person with no history of alcoholism in the immediate family. Research suggests that certain genes can increase the risk of alcoholism but which genes are involved or how they exert their influence in this regard remains controversial. Psychological factors may include a need for relief from anxiety, ongoing depression, unresolved conflict within relationships, or low self-esteem. Social factors include the availability of alcohol, social acceptance of the use of alcohol, peer pressure, and stressful lifestyles.

5.4. Diagnostic Guidelines for Alcohol Dependence

Given the serious health and social consequences of addiction it is prudent to be on the lookout for signs of emerging alcohol addiction. If the condition is diagnosed early enough it is often easier to take successful corrective measures. Those who are drifting towards habitual drinking show the following symptoms:

1) They have a strong desire to drink alcohol, and need a drink every day.
2) They often like to drink by themselves.
3) They may need a drink to stop the shakes.
4) Most drink early, usually first thing in the morning.
5) They spend considerable time in activities where alcohol is available such as a social club or pub.
6) They neglect other interests or pleasures because of alcohol drinking.

A definite diagnosis of alcohol dependence should usually be made only if three or more of the following have been experienced or exhibited at some time during the previous year:

1) A strong desire or sense of compulsion to drink alcohol.
2) Difficulties in controlling alcohol-consumption in terms of its onset, termination, or levels of use.
3) Characteristic physiological withdrawal symptoms are observed whenever alcohol use is reduced or stopped. The need to use of the alcohol to alleviate withdrawal symptoms.
3) Evidence of alcohol tolerance, such that increased doses are needed to achieve the same physiological effects (or intoxication) originally produced by the lower doses. Examples of this are found in alcohol-dependent individuals who may resort to doses sufficient to incapacitate or even kill a regular person.
4) A progressive neglect of alternative pleasurable activities or interests because of alcohol use.

5) Persisting with alcohol abuse despite clear evidence of serious harmful consequences, such as liver damage from excessive drinking.

5.5. What Can Help Me to Reduce or Stop Drinking?

Reversing alcoholism, though not easy, is certainly achievable and is easier to do in the beginning stages of the disease. To be assured of success one has to be fully committed and be determined to cure oneself. The practical approach is a stepwise solution.

Accepting the problem: Most alcoholics start out by denying to themselves and to others that they have a drinking problem. Accepting that a problem exists and deciding to seek some form of help are often a key step in overcoming the problem.

Self help: Some can be helped to overcome alcoholism by being better informed via books, websites, information and their own determination. Surprisingly, about 1 in 3 people with the problem do return to sensible drinking, or even cut it out completely, without the need for any professional help.

Seeking treatment: Some alcoholics may need to be helped by a professional nurse or doctor. Medical professionals can help one talk through the issues and causes related to alcoholism in more detail and help plan to manage drinking.

Treating other illnesses: In many cases, people turn to alcohol to better handle stress, anxiety, depression, or other mental health problems. However, the effect is short-lived and drinking increasing amounts of alcohol often makes these conditions worse.

5.6. Alcohol Use During Pregnancy

Consuming alcohol during pregnancy is strongly discouraged and presents a serious health risk to both the mother and the fetus. Alcohol in the blood system affects the physiological and cognitive development of the fetus. This is especially true in the early stages of pregnancy. Fetal alcohol syndrome (FAS), a devastating birth defect involving neurobehavioral and developmental abnormalities, is a typical example of a possible consequence alcohol abuse during pregnancy. Hundreds of individuals live with this debilitating disease though it is widely recognized as the most preventable fetal health risk. Although most studies of FAS pinpoint long-term heavy use of alcohol as its cause, scientific evidence also suggests that even a single drinking session of 5 or 6 drinks during early pregnancy might be enough to cause mental retardation and many of the facial defects associated with fetal alcohol syndrome. The American College of Obstetricians and Gynecologists (ACOG) recommends complete abstinence from alcohol during pregnancy.

Chapter 6: Your Health Today – Epilogue

Saké is a great refreshing beverage, an essential aspect of our day-to-day life and culture. It is made from organically grown best varieties of rice, naturally contains many wholesome and nutritious ingredients. Saké not only serves as a scrumptious beverage but also promotes both physical and mental health, prompts conversation and facilitates good social interactions helping people get along better with each other.

A phrase from a Kyogen play of the Muromach period (1338-1573) says that saké has 10 virtues. They are:

1) Saké can be better for your health than any medicine.
2) Saké will enable you to live longer.
3) Saké will recover you from fatigue and weariness.
4) Saké will drive gloom away and cheer you up.
5) You can make friends with anyone over a drink of saké.
6) Saké will create the atmosphere where everyone can express their opinions frankly (even to their superiors or seniors).
7) Saké is a good friend of those who live alone.
8) Saké will make you feel warm to endure cold weather.
9) Saké can serve as a versatile but nourishing meal during a trip.
10) Saké will be a great gift when you visit friends.

Recently, several consensus groups have concluded that moderate alcohol consumption reduces the overall risk of cardiovascular disease, cancer, dementia, osteoporosis and all-cause mortality. This is widely attributed to the variety and quantity of diverse amino acids present in saké. It has the highest amino acid content of any alcoholic beverage. This is perhaps why those who enjoy saké have a significantly lower risk of conditions such as liver cancer cirrhosis, and other cancers, compared to those who consume other types of alcoholic beverages.

In this work I have presented both the beneficial as well as risky aspects of saké. Both as a medical doctor and a regular daily drinker of saké, all I can recommend is that if you drink, then drink in moderation. Moderation with saké means one drink a day for women and one or two drinks a day for men. There is no doubt that excessive consumption of even saké can damage your health. Like with most drugs the health risks associated with alcohol are dose dependant. What is beneficial in moderation can easily be harmful when taken in excess and can eventually lead to liver damage, lead to cause various cancers, boost high blood pressure, trigger so-called bleeding (hemorrhagic) strokes, progressively weaken the heart muscle, scramble the brain and even harm unborn children.

While I fully acknowledge these probable problems with alcohol, I think it is also important to point out its potential benefits to middle-aged and older people. If presently you don't drink alcohol, you shouldn't feel compelled to start now because of the health benefits alone. One can get similar benefits by beginning a regimen of exercise or boosting the intensity and duration of your present physical activity. But if you are an adult with no history of depression or alcoholism who is at high risk for heart disease, a daily drink of saké may help reduce that risk. When the first reports appeared linking moderate alcohol consumption with lower rates of heart disease, many scientists thought that some other habit shared by drinkers, not the alcohol itself, accounted for the benefit. Today the scientific evidence strongly points out that alcohol itself is responsible for these benefits.

Bibliography

Related References

Alcohol Abuse and Alcoholism: Alcohol and the Cardiovascular System. Washington, DC: U.S. Department of Health and Human Services (1996).

Berger, K., et al., Light-to-moderate alcohol consumption and risk of stroke among US male physicians, New England Journal of Medicine, 341 (21), 1557-1564, 1999.

Blackwelder, W. C., et al., Alcohol and mortality. The Honolulu Heart Study, American Journal of Medicine, 68 (2), 164-169, 1980.

Boffetta, P. and Garefinkel, L., Alcohol drinking among men enrolled in an American Cancer Society prospective study. Epidemiology, 1 (5), 42-48, 1990.

Brenner, H., et al., The association between alcohol consumption and all-cause mortality in a cohort of male employees in the German construction industry, International Journal of Epidemiology, 26, 85-91, 1997.

Britton, A. and McPherson, K., Mortality in England and Wales attributable to current alcohol consumption. Journal of Epidemiology and Community Health, 55 (6), 383-388, 2001.

Cabot, R. C., The relation of alcohol to arteriosclerosis, Journal of the American Medical Association, 43, 774-775, 1904.

Calcoya, M., et al., Alcohol and Stroke: a community case control study in Asturias, Spain. Journal of Clinical Epidemiology, 52, 577-684, 1999.

Camargo, C. A., et al., Prospective study of moderate alcohol consumption and mortality in US male physicians. Archives of Internal Medicine, 157, 79-85, 1997.

Camargo, C. A., et al., Moderate alcohol consumption and the risk for angina pectoris or myocardial infarction in U.S. male physicians. Archives of Internal Medicine, 126 (5), 1997.

Coate, D., Moderate drinking and coronary heart disease mortality: evidence from NHANES I and NHANES I follow-up. American Journal of Public Health, 83 (6), 888-890, 1993.

Dairdron, D. M., Cardiovascular effects of alcohol. Western Journal of Medicine, 151 (4), 430-439, 1989.

Doll, R., et al., Mortality in relation to consumption of alcohol: 13 years observations on male British doctors. British Medical Journal, 309, 911-918, 1994.

Ellison, R. C., Does Moderate Alcohol Consumption Prolong Life? New York: American Council on Science and Health (1993).

Farchi, G., et al., Alcohol and survival in the Italian rural cohorts of the Seven Countries Study. International Journal of Epidemiology, 29, 667-671, 2000.

Fuchs, C. S., et al., Alcohol consumption and mortality among women. The New England Journal of Medicine, 332 (19), 1245-1250, 1995.

Gaziano, J. M., Alcohol and coronary heart disease. BELLE (Biological Effects of Low Level Exposures) Newsletter, 4 (1), 1-5, 1995.

Gronbaek, M., et al., Type of alcohol consumed and mortality from all causes, coronary heart disease, and cancer. Annals of Internal Medicine, 133 (6), 411-419, 2000.

Gronbaek, M., et al., Alcohol and mortality: is there a U-shaped relation in elderly people? Age and Aging, 27 (6), 739-744, 1998.
Gronbaek, M., et al., Influence of sex, age, body mass index, and smoking on alcohol intake and mortality, British Medical Journal, 308, 302-306, 1994.
Gronbaek, M., et al., Mortality associated with moderate intakes of wine, beer, or spirits, British Medical Journal, 310, 1165-1169, 1995.
Hennekens, C. H., Alcohol and Risk of Coronary Events. In: National Institute on
Hoffmeister, H., et al., The relationship between alcohol consumption, health indicators, and mortality in the German population. International Journal of Epidemiology, 28 (6), 1066-1072, 1999.
Keil, U., et al., The relation of alcohol intake to coronary heart disease and all-cause mortality in a beer drinking population, Epidemiology, 8 (2), 150-156, 1997.
Klatsky, A., Alcohol and mortality: a ten year Kaiser Permanente experience, Annals of Internal Medicine, 95, 139-145, 1981.
LaPorte, R. E. et al., The relationship of alcohol consumption to atherosclerotic heart disease. Preventive Medicine, 9, 22-40, 1980.
Lin, Y., et al., Alcohol consumption and mortality among middle-aged and elderly Japanese men and women. Ann Epidemiology, 15, 590-5907, 2005.
McCallum, J., et al*.,* The Dubbo Study of the Health of the Elderly 1988-2002: An Epidemiological Study of Hospital and Residential Care*. 9, 184-188, 1998; Sydney, NSW, Australia: The Australian Health Policy Institute (2003).*
Maskarinec, G., et al, Alcohol intake, body weight, and mortality in a multiethnic prospective cohort. Epidemiology, 9 (6), 654-661, 1998.
Moore, R. D. and Pearson, T. A., Moderate alcohol consumption and coronary artery disease. Medicine, 65, 242-267, 1986.
Nunokawa, Y., "Saké". In Rice Chemistry and Technology, American association of Cereal Chemists, Inc. (1972).
Ozasa, K., Alcohol use and mortality in the Japan Collaborative Cohort Study for evaluation of cancer. Asian Pacific Journal of Cancer Prevention, 8 (JACC Supplement), 81-87, 2008.
Perdue, L. and Shoemaker, W., The French Paradox and Beyond. Sonoma, CA: Renaissance Publishing (1992).
Renaud, S., et al., Alcohol and mortality in middle-aged men from eastern France. Epidemiology, 9, 184-188, 1998.
Renaud, S. and De Lorgeril, M., Wine, Alcohol, Platelets and the French Paradox for Coronary Heart Disease. Lancet (1), 1523-1526, 1992.
Rimm, E., et al., Prospective study of alcohol consumption and risk of coronary disease in men. Lancet, 338, 464-468, 1991.
Rimm, E., et al., Prospective study of cigarette smoking, alcohol use and the risk of diabetes in men. British Medical Journal, 310, 555-559, 1995.
Rimm, E., et al., Moderate alcohol intake and lower risk of coronary heart disease: meta-analysis of effects on lipids and hemostatic factors. British Medical Journal, 319, 1523-1528, 1999.
Rodgers, H., et al., Alcohol and Stroke: a case control study of drinking habits past and present. Stroke, 12 (10), 1473-1477, 1993.

Sacco, R. I., et al., The protective effect of moderate alcohol consumption on ischemic stroke. JAMM, 281, 55-60, 1999.
Stampfer, M., et al., Effects of moderate alcohol consumption on cognitive function in women. New English Journal of Medicine, 352, 245-253, 2005.
Truelsen, T., et al., Intake of beer, wine and spirits and risk of Stroke: the Copenhagen city heart study. Stroke, 29 (12), 2468-2472, 1998.
Wang, L., et al., Predictors of functional change: a longitudinal study of nondemented people aged 65 and older. Journal of the American Geriatrics Society, 50 (9), 1525-1534, 2002.
Willett, W. C. with the assistance of others., Eat, Drink, and Be Healthy: The Harvard Medical School Guide to Healthy Eating. New York: Simon & Schuster (2001).
Yuan, J-M., et al., Follow up study of moderate alcohol intake and mortality among middle aged men in Shanghai, China. British Medical Journal, 314, 18-23, 1997.

Recommended Reading

Japan Saké Brewers Association: Saké – The Making and Tradition of Japan's National Beverage (1998).
Gauntner, J., Saké World. http://www.Saké-world.com/home/.html
Kondo, H., Saké; A Drinker's Guide. Tokyo, New York, London, Kodansha International Ltd. (1984).
Oki Daikichi Honten, Expressing a dream of slow food and Saké, Japan's Arts Culture Magazine "Kateigaho", No 6, 2005.
Harper, P., The Insider's Guide to Saké. Kodansha International Ltd. (1998).
Shima-System Co. Ltd, JO-CON, E-mail: <info@jo-con.jp>
Takizawa, Y., Saké makes you healthy and vigorous every day, What's Nada no Saké? Health & Beauty, Story 1, pp. 2-6 (2006).

Index